Bloom's

GUIDES

Arthur Miller's
Death of a Salesman
New Edition

The Adventures of
   Huckleberry Finn
All the Pretty Horses
Animal Farm
The Autobiography of Malcolm X
The Awakening
The Bell Jar
Beloved
Beowulf
Black Boy
The Bluest Eye
Brave New World
The Canterbury Tales
Catch-22
The Catcher in the Rye
The Chosen
The Crucible
Cry, the Beloved Country
Death of a Salesman
Fahrenheit 451
A Farewell to Arms
Frankenstein
The Glass Menagerie
The Grapes of Wrath
Great Expectations
The Great Gatsby
Hamlet
The Handmaid's Tale
Heart of Darkness
The House on Mango Street
I Know Why the Caged Bird Sings
The Iliad
Invisible Man
Jane Eyre

The Joy Luck Club
The Kite Runner
Lord of the Flies
Macbeth
Maggie: A Girl of the Streets
The Member of the Wedding
The Metamorphosis
Native Son
Night
1984
The Odyssey
Oedipus Rex
Of Mice and Men
One Hundred Years of Solitude
Pride and Prejudice
Ragtime
A Raisin in the Sun
The Red Badge of Courage
Romeo and Juliet
The Scarlet Letter
A Separate Peace
Slaughterhouse-Five
Snow Falling on Cedars
The Stranger
A Streetcar Named Desire
The Sun Also Rises
A Tale of Two Cities
Their Eyes Were Watching God
The Things They Carried
To Kill a Mockingbird
Uncle Tom's Cabin
The Waste Land
Wuthering Heights

Bloom's
GUIDES

Arthur Miller's
Death of a Salesman
New Edition

Edited & with an Introduction
by Harold Bloom

BLOOM'S
LITERARY CRITICISM
An imprint of Infobase Publishing

Bloom's Guides: Death of a Salesman—New Edition
Copyright © 2011 by Infobase Publishing
Introduction © 2011 by Harold Bloom

Bloom's Literary Criticism
An imprint of Infobase Publishing
132 West 31st Street
New York NY 10001

Library of Congress Cataloging-in-Publication Data
Arthur Miller's Death of a salesman / edited and with an introduction by Harold Bloom. — New ed.
  p. cm. — (Bloom's guides)
  Includes bibliographical references and index.
  ISBN 978-1-60413-875-7 (acid-free paper)
  1. Miller, Arthur, 1915–2005. Death of a salesman. I. Bloom, Harold.
  II. Title: Death of a salesman.
  PS3525.I5156D4334 2011
  812'.52—dc22
                              2010027238

Contributing editor: Portia Williams Weiskel
Cover designed by Takeshi Takahashi
Composition by IBT Global, Troy NY
Cover printed by Yurchak Printing, Landisville, Pa.
Book printed and bound by Yurchak Printing, Landisville, Pa.

Printed in the United States of America

Contents

Introduction

HAROLD BLOOM

The dramatic critic Eric Bentley defines the central flaw in *Death of a Salesman* as Arthur Miller's inability (and consequently ours) to know whether the play's obsessive concern is politics or sex. Bentley's point is accurate, and the assertions of some feminist critics that Willy Loman's tragedy centers on "the politics of sex" seem to me unpersuasive. As a playwright, Arthur Miller works always in the shadow of Henrik Ibsen, a dangerous influence for Miller because Ibsen essentially was a daemonic dramatist, trollish and Shakespearean, always closer to a cosmos of elemental forces, like those in *King Lear* and *Macbeth*, than to the social world of politics and economics. Even Ibsen's social dramas conceal trollish energies behind their societal masks; Hedda Gabler is more a troll than a victim of the patriarchy and can be regarded as Iago's sister. But Miller always has imitated what he interprets as a social reformer in Ibsen, forgetting James Joyce's wry observation that Ibsen was no more a feminist than Joyce was a bishop. Social forces certainly affect Hedda Gabler, but Ibsen does not represent them as controlling her life or as determining her fate. Miller, in contrast, wants to give us a Willy Loman who is destroyed by social energies. Fortunately for the continued dramatic validity of *Death of a Salesman*, something deeper than Miller's political polemic pervades the play and makes it more than a parody of "the American Dream" of upward mobility, so that Willy Loman finally escapes the dubious fate of being a poor man's Jay Gatsby.

For a dramatic protagonist to impress us as legitimately "tragic," she or he must possess aesthetic dignity, which is not necessarily identical with human dignity. All bad tragedies, as Oscar Wilde might have said, are sincere, and Arthur Miller's sincerity is palpable. Miller has written some bad tragedies, but *Death of a Salesman* certainly is not one of them. With all its faults and ambiguities, it rivals Eugene O'Neill's *Long Day's Journey into Night* as a modern American tragic drama, even though, like O'Neill's work, it seems to me of a lesser eminence than the best tragicomedies of Tennessee Williams. Like O'Neill, Miller essentially is the tragedian of what Sigmund Freud called "family romances." *Death of a Salesman* is more the tragedy of a family than it is of an individual or of a society. Doubtless I am influenced by the experience of once having attended a performance of the play in Yiddish translation, which I found to be both illuminating and harrowing, though highly ironic, since Miller labors in his drama to render Willy as the American Everyman and the Lomans as an archetypal American family. Perhaps Miller succeeds in this effort, though at a certain cost, by blending Willy and the Lomans into a common grayness, so that they lack all color or exuberance and yield much of their pathos to a vision of social reductiveness, as if they were victims purely of the false dreams of their nation. What *Death of a Salesman* most lacks is a Shakespearean or Ibsenite foregrounding: a sense of the involvement of tradition both in Willy's loneliness and in his family's inability to understand his yearning quality, his dream of an excessive familial love that might assuage his loneliness.

Even though Willy Loman's aesthetic dignity depends more upon pathos than upon a nonexistent tragic grandeur, his dignity seems to me real enough to have sustained the play and to go on sustaining it for some years to come. Miller's social ironies mostly weaken the drama, yet the ironies of familial love in *Death of a Salesman* constitute its ongoing strength. Though it is more than 50 years since I saw the play in its Yiddish version, I remain seared by the peculiar power of that performance, which accentuated the anguish of the Lomans' family romance and the dignity of Willy's desperate failure to be what he yearned to be, a good father and a good husband. If Willy has tragic stature, it is because he is exiled from himself and so can win no victory whatsoever. We are terribly moved by Willy's confused conviction that, if he is not successful, then he will not deserve to be loved by his family. No possible success could assuage Willy's tormented yearning to be popular, to be loved. It is a peculiar tragedy that Willy is destroyed by love and by the inevitable ambivalences that attend family romances. The American Dream in Jay Gatsby is a High Romantic vision of Eros, grotesquely represented by his nostalgia for the banal Daisy, and yet still an authentic vision, because Gatsby himself, as mediated by the narrator Nick Carraway, is anything but banal. Willy Loman's American dream is rescued from aesthetic banality precisely because it is possessed by the enigmas that mark a guilty dream. Poor Willy, who desired so intensely only to be a good husband and a good father, destroys himself because of the guilty realization that pragmatically he has become both a bad husband and a bad father. I do not think that Willy Loman has the authentic dignity of a tragic protagonist, but his sincere pathos does have authentic aesthetic dignity, because he does not die the death of a salesman. He dies the death of a father, perhaps not the universal father, but a father central enough to touch the anguish of the universal.

Biographical Sketch

Born in Manhattan on October 17, 1915, Arthur Miller was
the second of three children for Isadore and Augusta Miller, a
well-to-do Jewish couple. In 1929 the stock market crash and
Depression forced his father out of the coat business and their
family out of their home to a small frame house in Brooklyn.
Upon graduating from Abraham Lincoln High School in 1932,
Miller started saving as much as he could from his income at an
auto parts warehouse so he could go to college. He occasionally
would read on the subway on his way to work, and when he
happened upon Dostoevsky's *The Brothers Karamazov*, Miller
"all at once believed [he] was born to be a writer."

But when he applied to the University of Michigan, Miller
was turned down until he tried for a third time with a convincing
letter he sent to the admissions officer. Having heard the school
gave writing prizes, he enrolled in journalism, and within 18
months he began writing plays, winning the Avery Hopwood
Award on his first try for a piece he had written in just four days,
Honors at Dawn. He received another Hopwood for his second
work, *No Villain*, just one year later in 1937.

After he received his B.A. in 1938, Miller went back to New
York and worked with the Federal Theatre Project until it was
abolished; he then ended up on welfare. He completed his play,
The Golden Years, and to make money he wrote numerous radio
scripts—work he hated. In 1940 Miller married Mary Grace
Slattery, to whom he had become engaged at the University
of Michigan; they moved to Brooklyn and eventually had two
children. He held various odd jobs and kept writing for the next
four years, while she served as the main breadwinner, working
as a waitress and editor.

In 1944, his first Broadway production took place. The play's
title, *The Man Who Had All the Luck*, certainly wasn't applicable
to Miller at the time, for the piece struggled through only six
performances, although it managed to win the Theatre Guild
National Award. A back injury kept Miller out of the military,
but he visited army camps during the war and published his

journal, *Situation Normal*, in 1944. By 1945 Miller switched gears and wrote a novel, *Focus*, about anti-Semitism. He became increasingly involved in leftist organizations and liberal causes. Then in 1947 his first son was born, and his first successful Broadway play was produced, *All My Sons*. It showed the after-effects of World War II on a family whose father had sold faulty plane parts to the government.

But Miller's most famous play by far became *Death of a Salesman*, which centered on a dejected salesman's final days. It was composed in six weeks on a typewriter Miller had bought with the money he earned from his first Hopwood. That year, 1949, the Pulitzer Prize was awarded—for the first time—to Miller. He also received the New York Drama Critics' Circle Award for the work, which continued through 1950 for 742 performances. The same year Miller traveled to California to work on a film project. He met Marilyn Monroe and they saw each other frequently for many weeks.

In 1951 Miller published an adaptation of Henrik Ibsen's *An Enemy of the People*. Political commitments took up much of Miller's time then, and in 1953 he put his warnings about the dangers of mass hysteria and government power into the form of *The Crucible*, a work about the Salem witch trials that was readily construed as a metaphor for the McCarthy hearings then taking place. By 1955 Miller's marriage was falling apart, and he met Monroe again at a theater party. They were seen together more often, and he was divorced that year. Miller married Marilyn Monroe in 1956.

The Crucible was well received, but it helped bring Miller negative attention of another sort. In June of 1956 he was subpoenaed to appear before the House Un-American Activities Committee. Curiously, in the midst of his political troubles, he announced that he and Monroe had been secretly married. Before the committee, Miller freely admitted his past associations with leftist groups, stating they had ended in 1950. He went further and refused to be a "good citizen" who would identify other communists. He named not one.

During this time, in 1955, Miller saw his *A View from the Bridge* produced on a double bill with a short play, *A Memory of Two Mondays*. He also won his second Pulitzer Prize. His screenplay for the 1961 film *The Misfits* was created for his wife, who starred in it with Clark Gable, but shortly thereafter in that same year, they were divorced. Also in that year, Miller's mother died at the age of 80.

In 1962, Miller married the photographer Inge Morath, with whom he had two children and collaborated on several books, writing text to accompany her images. By 1964, Miller's *After the Fall* was produced, creating more controversy than any of his previous work. Many critics balked at what they construed to be an excessively autobiographical piece.

Miller covered the Nazi trials in Frankfurt for the *New York Herald Tribune* and then wrote *Incident at Vichy* (1965), a short play about Nazism and anti-Semitism in Vichy France. In the same year he traveled extensively in Europe to oversee productions of his various works.

In 1966 approximately 17 million viewers saw *Death of a Salesman* on television, 20 times the number who had seen the play when it was on Broadway. A collection of short stories, *I Don't Need You Anymore* (1967), followed, and another play, *The Price* (1968). He was a member of the Connecticut delegation to the fateful Democratic National Convention in 1972, and he continued to be politically active and speak out for his beliefs. In 1973 the comic *The Creation of the World and Other Business* was produced, as well as *The Archbishop's Ceiling* (1977) and *The American Clock* (1980).

In 1983 Miller directed *Death of a Salesman* in China. *Up from Paradise* was published in 1984, followed by *Danger: Memory!* in 1986, and his autobiography, *Timebends: A Life*, in 1987. He continued to see his works published and produced not only in theater but also on television. In 1994 *Broken Glass* was published, and in 1995 production began on a film version of *The Crucible*.

Dustin Hoffman, one of the most famous Willy Lomans, describes Miller in *Arthur Miller and Company* as "so articulate. He's this great storyteller. He sounds like this New York cab driver; he's so unpretentious and earthy. You're laughing one minute, then you're thinking the next, and touched the next." Arthur Miller died at his Connecticut home on February 10, 2005.

The Story Behind the Story

During a rehearsal of *Death of a Salesman* in Beijing using Chinese actors for a Chinese audience, Arthur Miller suddenly stood up, stopped the play, and made a speech to all assembled about his feelings for the character of Willy Loman. Miller was pleased by the progress of actor Ying Ruocheng's portrayal of Willy as " . . . a little bantam with quick fists and the irreducible demand that life give him its meaning and significance and honor." (*"Salesman" in Beijing* 49) But he was disappointed that the entire company had not yet succeeded in animating the poetic vision of the play. He quotes himself:

> . . . [T]he one red line connecting everyone in the play was a love for Willy; not admiration necessarily, but a kind of visceral recognition that in his fumbling and often ridiculous way he is trying to lift up a belief in immense redeeming possibilities. (49)

Acknowledging that Willy was often irascible and not always deserving of emulation, Miller articulated what has become the most common response to his most famous character: "[Willy] is the walking believer, the bearer of a flame whose going-out would leave us flat." (49)

By the time Miller arrived in China to direct his play (1983), *Salesman* had been playing continuously to appreciative audiences since its opening on February 10, 1949, at the Morosco Theatre in New York City. The play instantly generated controversy, focusing mainly on two questions: Can the classical definitions of tragedy—persons of great stature and elevated consciousness brought down by a combination of fate and personal flaw—be properly expanded and updated to include the suffering and downfall of Willy Loman, indisputably a common man? And, can the play be understood as an indictment of American capitalism? Although Miller has commented extensively on these issues, his interest in the play has tended more to the question of its universality.

Recent feminist criticism has questioned whether the perceived marginalization of women in the play—especially Linda—both dates and diminishes the work, but Miller was attempting to accurately reflect the times, and in any case his question still stands: Is Willy's story emblematic of a human aspiration recognizable to people of all nations? This was the challenge that brought him to Beijing.

Salesman had played successfully to many foreign audiences, but the desecration of art carried out in the Cultural Revolution by Mao's wife Jiang Qing and the Gang of Four had left an entire generation of Chinese bereft of any awareness of world literature or culture. Theater people like Ruocheng were banished to rice farms, leaving the people with Jiang Qing's simplistic "Eight Permissible Plays." If one in four human beings is Chinese, Miller reminds us, hope for "universality" must confront alien concepts and daunting difficulties with translations. Miller struggled with transmitting culture-bound concepts like the link between suicide and insurance money for Biff and had to accept Willy's impassioned, "I won't take the rap for this" to be translated, "I won't carry this blackened cooking pot on my back." In the end, however, despite a few alarmed moments of anticipating that "the whole effort would end in calamity" (viii), Miller and his Chinese colleagues produced *Salesman* to an appreciative Chinese audience. Full of emotion, the audience responded with prolonged applause and did not seem to care that the last buses home were leaving without them. Miller was exhilarated to have this confirmation of his belief in one humanity.

Interestingly, in no other play except Wilder's *Our Town* do American dreams, contradictions, and history figure so centrally. June Schleuter's essay in *Approaches to Teaching Miller's "Death of a Salesman"* provides a useful chronology. Willy was born in 1886, and his brother Ben was born in 1873. In 1880, their father deserted the family, heading to Alaska, not to be seen again. The Loman family drama is rooted in the myth and reality of the American West when it was still possible to wander without destination, seeking to subdue the land and claim its riches for one's own.

14

Willy grounded his life in a different success myth, historically associated with Horatio Alger's rags-to-riches novels that would have been selling by the millions during Willy's formative years. Building on Ben Franklin's cheery certainty that hard work, discipline, and character would lead to personal success ("The Way to Wealth" speech in *Poor Richard's Almanack*, 1758) and Emerson's essay "Self-Reliance" (1841), Alger, a clergyman, expanded the myth to include the dubious but liberating notion that achieving material success was God's intention for humankind. American identity—both spiritual and public—was engaged by this mythology. "Success is a requirement Americans make of life," wrote critic Henry Popkin, mentioning Willy. (Henry Popkin, *Sewanee Review* LXVII. Winter, 1960, p. 53)

The American Dream functions almost like a character in *Salesman*, but in the words of critic Thomas E. Porter:

> Miller uses this [American Dream] model in order to subvert it. His play is an anti-myth, the rags-to-riches formula in reverse so that it becomes the story of a failure in terms of success, or better, the story of the failure of the success myth. (Porter 131)

This darker side of American life received less publicity than the success myth but was the inevitable consequence of postwar capitalist competition in an expanding economy. For some to win in this system, others had to lose. And for readers interested in overlapping explanations for Willy's failures, images from the Depression are instructive. Miller recalled for a BBC interview in 1995 three Depression-era suicides on his Brooklyn block. "These people," he said, "were profound believers in the American Dream. The day the money stopped their identity was gone." (Qf. *The Cambridge Companion to Arthur Miller* 1)

Two Americans—one in anticipation, the other in retrospection—seemed to have had in mind a person like Willy Loman when writing about the American experience. Thoreau's early lines in *Walden* (1854)—"The mass of men lead lives of quiet desperation"—evoke an image of Willy as we might imagine him spending a lifetime of bone-wearying hours in his car or hotel room, planning his next move, figuring his day's commission. And Willy with his social awkwardness, self-doubt, and abruptly changing emotional states fits David Riesman's description in *The Lonely Crowd* (1969) of the "inner-directed" person trying to fit into an "other-directed" society. Riesman described the subsequent loss of personhood and mental disintegration as "anomie." Both observations shed light on Willy's poignant and memorable self-description to his older brother Ben: " . . . I still feel kind of temporary about myself."

Salesman came into being almost overnight. In the summer of 1948 Miller was working fitfully on another play when suddenly, from several unrelated parts of his life, a stream of images and ideas coalesced into a play about a salesman. The original title—"The Inside of His Head"—reflected Miller's intention to present a drama of personal downfall from a purely subjective viewpoint, but it was abandoned after he found himself engaged in more complex themes.

The compelling script attracted the attention of Elia Kazan, the famous director who had just concluded a successful run of Tennessee Williams's *A Streetcar Named Desire*. Several commentators have enjoyed reporting on the elaborate efforts made by Mildred Dunnock, a slight and elegant actress, to win the part of Linda, pictured by Miller as dowdy, like one who lived in her housedress. Lee J. Cobb was the first "Willy." To impart the dignity and gravity deemed appropriate to the "Willy" character, Miller and Kazan took Cobb to a performance of Beethoven's Seventh Symphony the afternoon of *Salesman*'s first performance. Despite warnings from some promoters that the title was too morose to attract—and might even repel—audiences, the play ran for 742 performances. It won that year's Pulitzer Prize and numerous other awards and put Arthur Miller firmly on the American scene.

List of Characters

Arthur Miller tells us that **Willy Loman** has a mercurial nature and turbulent dreams. Son Happy tells us that Willy is happiest when looking forward to something. Linda likens him to "only a little boat looking for a harbor." To her, he is "the dearest man in the world . . . [and] the handsomest." To son Biff, Willy is both a "prince" and a "phony little fake." Willy indignantly insists that he is "not a dime a dozen"; but he also feels "kind of temporary about [himself]." The question of the play is: Who is Willy and why does his life turn out as it does? Fatherless father of Biff and Happy, husband of Linda, Willy is the (not especially talented) traveling salesman responsible for the New England territories. His characteristic bravado masks a disabling insecurity that drives him to make fanciful claims—the Providence police personally protect his parked car, for example—and to live vicariously through his sons, especially Biff, his favorite. Now in his sixties, stoop-shouldered and exhausted, Willy is hours away from being fired when we meet him and a few more hours away from planting seeds where no sun will shine and then taking his own life. The name "Willy Loman" has become almost synonymous with the American Dream—both the high hopes and the hopes dashed and all the energy associated with its attainment.

Biff Loman, the older of Willy's sons, moves from being the popular and promising high school football hero to a 34-year-old small-time thief and occasional farmhand. At the time of the play Biff is—and has been—struggling to put his life in order. Ambivalent about his father and therefore about himself, "lost" Biff faces the pressure of choosing a life and career that will satisfy his own nature or one that will win his father's approval. Some critics regard Biff's role in the play as equivalent to Willy's because Biff must consciously act on the issues and dilemmas that destroy his less-self-aware father. Certainly their destinies are intertwined. Emotionally paralyzed and fated to carry the family secret, Biff has nonetheless achieved sufficient self-knowledge to be able to dismiss Happy's description of him as "idealistic" in favor of the more truthful "mixed up very bad." The play does not condemn Biff for his impulse to whistle in elevators or go off swimming in the middle of the day. Ben Franklin would have worried about Biff, but Walt Whitman would have enjoyed his companionship.

Happy Loman, the younger son, not only does not whistle in elevators, but he castigates brother Biff for doing so because— he insists—such acts of spontaneous whimsy do not get one hired in the business world. In the shadow of Biff's high school glory, Happy is frequently seen—through Willy's recollected episodes—struggling for his father's attentions. As an adult, Happy has fallen unimaginatively (though with different illusions) into a self-gratifying version of Willy's career path. Both sons are tall, fit, and attractive to women, but Miller gives to Happy the role of exuding the sexuality that is otherwise a hidden and problematic theme in the play. Happy idealizes his mother and treats other women with callous bravado and self-indulgence. His concern for Willy prompts him to pay for a respite trip to Florida, but his refusal to publicly recognize his distraught father in the restaurant is an act of astonishing cruelty.

Linda Loman, wife and mother in the family, appears to take a passive role in the play, but she has generated her own share of controversial commentary, especially by critics. Some see her as admirable and selfless for taking the role encouraged for postwar women of returning to domestic life to provide stability and emotional support for the American family. Others see her as pathetic and marginalized (along with the other women in the play) by the male characters. Difficulty in understanding Linda is exacerbated by her reticence about herself. Aware in a way that the others are not of the precariousness of the family, she has understandably placed Willy's problems at the center of her life. Miller tells us she has an "iron repression," but does this indicate long-suffering love or resentment, exhaustion, a fierce will, or defeat? In Beijing Miller insisted that Linda be played as the kind of woman " . . . who is strong by concealing her strength." (*"Salesman"* *in Beijing* 87) Indisputable and unwavering is Linda's love for Willy, but some aspects of her behavior seem irrational and self-defeating: Why, for example, would one encourage a beloved spouse to continue in his exaggerations and self-deceptions? Despite her "I don't understand" speech at the grave site, Linda possesses more of the facts of the play than the other characters, and her "Attention must be paid" speech is among the most famous in American drama.

In Willy's delusional episodes his older brother, Ben (**Uncle Ben**), appears as a living character. We learn later that Ben has died, apparently fairly recently. His ghostly appearances during Willy's final days of life provide important insights about Willy's character and why he has become who he is. Director Elia Kazan persuaded Miller to change Ben's role to de-emphasize his influence on Willy as the stand-in father for their deserted family in order to amplify his sensational qualities as the embodiment of the American success myth. Ben is fabulously rich and more damaging than useful as a father replacement. Ben's signature lines—". . . [W]hen I was seventeen I walked into the jungle, and when I was twenty-one I walked out. And by God I was rich."—convey his rapacious opportunism. And his advice to Biff—"Never fight fair with a stranger, boy. You'll never get out of the jungle that way."—conveys his compromised ethics. Although we only know about Ben what Willy's selective memory presents, he appears to have misused the concept of "self-reliance" to justify his belligerent self-aggrandizement. Although married with children, Ben acts like one without emotional ties; he barely tolerates Willy, is plainly disdainful of Linda, and interacts with his nephews only by showing off his questionable ethics. Without Ben in the play, we would never know about Willy's origins, which are clearly implicated in the tormenting conflicts and confusion he has endured most of his life.

As Willy's longtime neighbor and friend, **Charley** is the unlikely poetic defender of the salesman's dreams and easy to characterize as the "decent capitalist" in the play. He appears to have played fair and been moderately successful. Charley has, however, and by his own admission, paid a price for his success: "My salvation is that I never took any interest in anything." Since Willy began faltering on the job, Charley has quietly been "loaning" him money to pay the bills and even offers him a job. He enjoys teasing Willy but always affectionately; no matter how exasperating Willy is, Charley remains a friendly and concerned neighbor. Charley's presence at the funeral as the only nonrelative in attendance harshly contrasts with the image carried by Willy all these years of the adoring admirers of legendary salesman Dave Singleman gathered for his funeral.

Son of Charley and friend, neighbor, and classmate of the Loman boys, **Bernard** provides a telling contrast to Biff. Never athletic in high school, "liked" but not "*well* liked," studious and conscientious, instead—these features, scorned by Willy and his boys at the time, turn out to have served Bernard well. While grown-up Biff is floundering, Bernard is a practicing lawyer with a case currently before the Supreme Court. Bernard also functions in the play as witness to Biff's unpromising characteristics in high school and to the traumatic effect on Biff of his fateful visit to Willy in Boston in the summer of 1932. Remarkably, although Bernard was frequently in the shadow of the Loman brothers, he has always exhibited more concern for them than resentment. He does, however, know that "You can't get something for nothing," as Biff does not.

Howard, son of Willy's original boss, has the brief but pivotal role of firing Willy just at the moment Willy is asking for the less strenuous job of non-traveling salesman. In this capacity Howard is often castigated as the callous capitalist, but he is also—and perhaps more disturbingly—an ordinary man, like Willy, a proud father of two. Willy has, in fact, not been performing well for the business, but it is difficult not to regard as an inexcusable cruelty Howard's oblivious disregard of Willy's desperate plight. Howard is mesmerized by his new gadget, the tape recorder, and so focused on protecting his "bottom line" that he doesn't appear even to see Willy. Willy, with his second-to-last hope, is eclipsed in this scene, reduced to nothing.

Summary and Analysis

Contribution of Stage Design to Theme

Only moments into the play we know the essential story: A salesman—not ill but clearly exhausted and discouraged, and introduced incongruously by pleasantly pastoral music—will die by the end of the play. Before the audience hears a word of dialogue, the stage design has provided this framework for Willy's life with the use of one auditory and one visual device. The auditory clue—the ". . . melody . . . played upon a flute . . . telling of grass and trees and the horizon"—contrasts harshly with the visual clue—the image of Willy's modest house menacingly dwarfed (again, the incongruity) by the "towering, angular" apartment buildings that now surround it. Someone accustomed to horizons and wide open spaces is likely inclined to think adventurously, even to dream of wild possibility. But one whose window "opens" onto a building that forms part of a "solid vault" of similar view-obstructing buildings is likely to feel like a caged spirit, like one not quite alive. Willy—we come to learn—is both of these people.

Director Elia Kazan said of Willy: "[He is] one vast contradiction . . . and this contradiction is his downfall." He and set designer Jo Mielziner joined their talents with Miller's to create a powerful and evocative setting that would reflect Willy's contradictory nature and dilemma. Miller's original stage image of a large head opening to reveal a "mass of contradictions" would have been an effective Expressionistic device for dramatizing a single disintegrating mind, but Miller's view of life and art precluded reducing a person to a disintegrating mind or human existence to a jumble of subjective experiences. The set as it finally evolved blended features of Realism and Expressionism with a result so rich in symbolism and significance, both emotional and historical, that critic Enoch Brater wrote, "In a very real sense, the set is Miller's play." (Brater 119) The stage design made possible the subjective enactment of Willy's suffering in a context that invited audiences to reflect on what objective historical and economic circumstances may have contributed to the downfall of this quite ordinary American citizen. Willy's house, for example, is not even his own, nor is his death. Both belong explicitly to a "salesman." Such a deliberate reference recalls the observation commonly made by native and foreign America-watchers alike that Americans think of themselves in terms of what they do; their identity is their job title. According to this view, the "real self" or "inner nature" is undervalued, even betrayed, in service to the profit-making economic system. English critic Raymond Williams articulates one version of this political view of *Salesman*:

> . . . in the end it is not Willy Loman as a man, but the image of the Salesman. . . . that sums up the theme referred to as alienation, for this is a man who from selling things has passed to selling himself, and has become, in effect . . . a commodity which like other commodities will at a certain point be economically discarded. (Corrigan, ed. 75)

From a related perspective, Miller scholar Linda Kintz points out the implied message of rejection located in the sight of Willy's little plot of earth and isolated domicile left behind by America's prideful urbanization. She writes:

> Built into that message is the inherent contradiction between an admonition to be number one, which Willy takes seriously, and the inevitability that there will be far more losers than winners, a message he hears only too late. (Bigsby, ed. 104)

In the introduction to his *Collected Plays*, Miller acknowledges that he intentionally left unclear what Willy was carrying in his salesman's bags ("Himself") but insists that no explicit political view or overt program for social reform motivated his writing the play. The set design is equally suited to dramatizing public and private issues and particularly the synergy created when they overlap. The varying musical themes closely follow Willy's inner state of mind. The "angry orange" and lonely blue colors on stage and the sheltering leafy overlay highlighting family life in Brooklyn before it became a claustrophobic "asphalt jungle" are subjective and objective indicators of Loman family life. The spatial juxtaposition of rooms on stage permits intimate and simultaneous views of Linda alone in her bedroom worrying about Willy—who is audibly mumbling to himself in the kitchen—while the grown sons briefly back together in their old bedroom engage in a disjointed conversation consisting of crude "guy talk" and alarm about their father. The kitchen table signifies American family life. The refrigerator that breaks down first because it is new and getting itself "worked in" and then because it is old evokes the era of time payments and frustration with cheap and falsely advertised gadgets. Biff's athletic trophy is now tellingly located not in the boys' room but in Willy's. The otherwise uncluttered stage leaves the most space for the dramatization of Willy's escalating madness.

Function of Time Sequences

Death of a Salesman consists of three parts, two acts and the Requiem, and encompasses three time sequences. The play opens and closes in historical time—the year 1949. Both acts blend this linear time scheme with fragments of past time which Willy not so much recalls as reenters to relive for purposes that serve both himself and the audience. The audience comes to understand that Willy's departures from linear time are a response to a deep need within himself for self-understanding. These episodes also make possible Miller's critical interest in providing the view from inside Willy's head. The characters' sometimes realistic, sometimes phantasmal actions around doors and walls are visible markers for the shifting time dimensions in Willy's mind. A third category of time is a nonsequential dimension. Episodes occurring in this category consist of merged fragments of past and present time that engulf Willy with increasing frequency and intensity as the boundaries in his mind dissolve. These skillfully constructed scenes provide external manifestations of Willy's mental disintegration and some clues about why it is occurring.

The Requiem, by contrast, provides the distance—locatable in objective time and space—from which Willy's survivors and the audience may ponder and comment upon the meaning of his death.

Willy's Crisis

Act 1 opens as Willy, dressed in his salesman's clothes, is returning home after another in a series of recently occurring failed business trips. His exhaustion and sense of defeat blend with Linda's barely suppressed alarm. Willy's return marks the beginning of the last day of his life. At the time, however, despite the air of urgency surrounding him, only Linda has reasons for premonition, and her days have been consumed with frantic strategies to save her husband's life.

Willy is a man carrying the weight of many losses. Miller describes him as coming home to "let his burden down," but coming home also brings him face to face with the most tormenting of his losses: his relationship with son Biff. Willy has lost his grip on life; he has literally lost his grip on his car, which seems to him to be steering itself off the road. Willy has just spent most of his day inside of it, lost and dangerously disoriented. The car—central symbol of success in American culture and of vital importance for a salesman—is no longer under Willy's control.

Willy's implausible excuse for his abnormal behavior—an odd cup of coffee—reveals how far he has strayed from his own senses. As we watch Linda's response to Willy in this first scene, we see she has joined him in his disordered thinking as well—maybe it's his glasses or the steering mechanism of the car—but she has done so to keep the appearance of normality when she knows otherwise. One may come to question the wisdom or appropriateness of Linda's interventions with Willy (or the absence of them), but she is clearly animated by a fierce and loyal love for her husband. Suggesting to Willy that taking an aspirin will help him feel better exposes her desperate state of mind. Linda is at the outer limit of her capacity to cope with Willy's condition. Other sources of help—professional or familial—that might have been available are, for reasons of history or personal fate, not available to her.

Also in this first scene, Willy exposes some elements of the pattern his desperation has taken: explosive bouts of self-contradiction (Biff is lazy, Biff is not lazy) and vacillation between defeat ("I just couldn't make it. . . .") and little spasms of feigned hope ("I'm vital in New England"). Within the latter comment one also hears the measure of Willy's self-deception. Using the only resources they can summon, Willy and Linda create a kind of false consciousness about the turmoil at the center of their lives.

Willy is unmistakably afflicted with many of the now classic signs of depression. He has lost his capacity for concentration and remembering; he cannot drive and confuses his current car with the one belonging to the family in 1928. But these are symptomatic losses pointing to far more disruptive losses in Willy's life. He speaks "with wonder" of the scenery and sunshine he encounters more abundantly the farther north—away from his home and the city—he travels. The simple pleasures of beauty and warmth put Willy into a reverie so deeply satisfying that he falls into a private mental region where there are no longer any cars or roads. The power of this reverie to put Willy's life in danger suggests that some vital inner deprivation has overtaken his conscious life. Indeed, evoked first by the flute music, a profound lament runs through the entire play for the loss of open space, a wide sky, and real earth under one's feet.

Once back in his house, Willy demands to have opened the already open windows; nothing can alleviate his sense of being "boxed in" with "windows and bricks." We readily infer that the Lomans were unable to afford the land next door and therefore impotent to save from destruction two well-loved elm trees by an impersonal, almost mechanical "they." Willy's "sense of place"—a defining ingredient of the American Dream experience observed by prominent scholars of American culture from de Tocqueville to Wendell Berry—has been violated. The degree of bitterness generated by this kind of loss is heard in Willy's choice of words: "They massacred the neighborhood."

"They" *have* massacred this neighborhood and thousands like it. But who is this "they"? Willy is right to connect this heart-wrenching loss to runaway population growth, but he has neither the intellect nor the self-awareness to recognize the contradiction inherent in his angry sadness—namely, that the material wealth promised by the American Dream, which Willy equates with "success," is delivered through the system of capitalism, which requires ever increasing growth in population and consumption. This in turn ensures the paving over of America, building lot by building lot, and the irrevocable loss of a profound source of personal happiness. No character in the play reflects directly on this paradox of American life—although each one is affected by it. Audiences and critics, however, do reflect on these and related issues raised by the play, and these observations are part of the once-heated and still ongoing commentary about the play. Miller, like the Greeks, wanted his plays to have a social impact without being polemical. In *Death of a Salesman* it's not a contest of ideas we are observing but rather the complexities of people's lives as they consciously and unconsciously embrace and resist the prevailing influences of the time.

Willy's keenest and most disabling loss is his relationship with son Biff. At the time of the play, 34-year-old Biff has returned home in nearly as much turmoil about starting a life as Willy is of concluding his. A shift of light focuses on Biff and Happy in their bedroom, both now out of bed, unable to sleep after overhearing the agitated talk coming from below. Their conversation exposes a genuine sibling bond despite the marked differences in their personalities. Also exposed are the remarkable similarities between Biff and his father. Like Willy, Biff is both driven and paralyzed, dominated by feelings of shame, guilt, anger, and determination. Both express an unsatisfied desire for connection to the land and open spaces. Biff can find satisfying work on a Texas ranch but finds himself each spring suddenly ensnared in self-doubt "about not gettin' anywhere!" Happy, by contrast, claims to enjoy the outdoor life, but his enthusiasm is compromised by male narcissism and an unapologetic preference for making money. Above all, Happy is eager for conquest and self-aggrandizement and appears indifferent about using callous and indecent means to make his impression. He imagines, for example, humiliating his merchandise manager by outboxing him in the middle of the store and boasts to Biff about seducing the soon-to-be bride of an executive of the business. Unlike Biff, Happy is self-deceived, naming his aggression "an overdeveloped sense of competition," and quick to idealize, calling "poetic" Biff's anguished speech about the newborn Texas colts, words Biff himself insists were "mixed up very bad." Both brothers are (with different emphasis) skeptical about equating happiness with wealth; they share (with equal emphasis) an expanding anxiety about Willy. Hints about a dark secret carried by Biff are introduced and hastily dropped in this scene.

What emerges in these early episodes is an unarticulated conflict between two American ideals: the pursuit of happiness through connection to the land (associated with homesteading and frontier life) and the pursuit of happiness associated with the acquisition of material wealth. As the play unfolds, we notice that the ethical systems governing each ideal are inherently incompatible. The ensuing conflict is reenacted especially acutely in Biff and Willy but generally in the whole family and by implication the whole nation.

Arthur Miller scholar M. C. Roudané points out the numerous instances in the play "in which Willy's body language and dialogue create images of the fall, the falling, or the fallen." (Bigsby, ed. 66) Our first impression of Willy is of a man on the verge of collapse. He "sinks" into a chair, appears "beaten down," and, in Act Two, is abandoned on the floor of a restaurant, "on his knees." As we absorb the accumulating weight of these images, we may also become aware of an invisible kind of falling: Willy's recurring lapses into other dimensions of time.

Miller's Use of Time in Act 1

American thinking has traditionally emphasized linear progress in the form of a belief in starting over and getting a second chance. Early manifestation of this thinking is found in the fervor the new settlers felt for overthrowing the old ways of England and Europe and in the notions of "rags to riches" and "Manifest Destiny." Some American writers have worked against this grain. One thinks of William Faulkner's famous line—"The past is not dead; it's not even past."—that occurs in a speech by the perspicacious narrator Gavin Stevens in *The Town* (1957) and F. Scott Fitzgerald's insight about the futility of trying to escape the past conveyed through the famous concluding images of *The Great Gatsby* (1925). Arthur Miller stands in this tradition of American writers. He studied the Greek playwrights and Henrik Ibsen during his college years and was impressed by their similar obsession with the "presentness" of the past. The objective events of *Salesman* are enacted over a period of 24 hours, but the play derives its intensity from the novel intermingling of past and present sequences of experience that create a sense of Willy Loman beyond chronological time. We are privileged in this manner to get as close as possible to the eternal nature of another human being.

In his introduction to *The Collected Plays*, Miller writes, "*Death of a Salesman* [is founded upon] the concept that nothing in life comes 'next' . . . everything exists together and at the same time within us; . . . there is no past to be 'brought forward' in a human being . . . he is in his past at every moment. . . ." (*Collected Plays* 23) An innovative artist, Miller saw the potential in blending the different representations of time used in expressionistic and realistic theater, that is to say, mingling sequences of subjective and chronological time, for dramatizing a more complete and genuine measure of human feeling. In *Arthur Miller and Company*, Miller states, "I've come out of the playwriting tradition which is Greek and Ibsen where the past is the burden of man and it's got to be placed on the stage so he can grapple with it." (*Arthur Miller and Company* 201) Earlier he stated, "[The] job of the artist is to remind people of what they have chosen to forget." (200)

When asked about his artistic methods of presenting time, Miller has frequently cited the pivotal moment in his career when he met by chance his Uncle Manny as both were emerging from a showing in Boston of *All My Sons*. Without even a greeting, Manny began to cry and then speak about his own son without any explicit reference to whatever in the play had churned up his thoughts. Miller called it "non-transitional speech" and immediately saw its poetic possibility for the theater. The episode had for Miller the quality of epiphany, and its impact explains the title he gave his 1987 autobiography—*Timebends*—where he writes:

> How fantastic a play would be that did not still the mind's simultaneity, did not allow a man to 'forget' and turned him to see present through past and past through present, a form that in itself, quite apart from its content and meaning, would be inescapable as a psychological process and as a collecting point for all that his life in society had poured into him. (*Timebends* 131)

Because time has a central importance for Miller in general and for this play in particular, more discussion of the issue is helpful. "Flashback" is the customary term for the technique of including scenes from the past to illustrate meaning in the present. But this is not what is happening to Willy. The action in the two acts moves in concert with Willy's wandering thoughts. On this point Elia Kazan wrote, "There are no flashbacks. . . . The only laws of these scenes are the laws of Willy's mind. And all the figures in Willy's mind are distorted by Willy's *hopes, wishes, desires*." (Rowe 44)

The presence of the past in the present disorders chronological time but does not make it less legitimate. Miller's integration of these memory sequences into the dialogue ("non-transitional speech") allows the audience to observe—and almost to experience—the way in which elements from Willy's past, both happy and ominous, combine with his increasingly frantic hopes for the future. The consequence for Willy is disorientation to the point of impotence. And it is exactly what we see: Willy unable to make anything happen—on the road; with his sons; with Linda, who disobeys his sharp command to throw out the torn stockings; and, in act 2, with his boss;

and out in his almost sunless little patch of backyard, trying to make seeds grow. The intensity of Willy's vacillation between euphoria and dismay deprives him of rational thought and self-control and makes of his present life a sustained torture of self-doubt and recrimination. Miller has effectively produced in this play a heightened sense of reality, of the full reality of Willy's state of mind in these moments: the dramatization of insanity. Miller has this to say about Willy in his lapses:

> [Willy] was the kind of man you see muttering to himself on a subway, decently dressed, on his way home or to the office, perfectly integrated with his surroundings excepting that unlike other people he can no longer restrain the power of his experience from disrupting the superficial sociality of his behavior. Consequently he is working on two logics which often collide. For instance, if he meets his son Happy while in the midst of some memory in which Happy disappointed him, he is instantly furious at Happy, despite the fact that Happy at this particular moment deeply desires to be of use to him. He is literally at that terrible moment when the voice of the past is no longer distant but quite as loud as the voice of the present. In dramatic terms the form, therefore, *is* this process, instead of being a once-removed summation or indication of it. (*Collected Works* 25–26)

Willy's Relived Memories

Critic Neil Carson points out that "Willy's memories do not materialize at random. They are triggered by certain incidents in the present, and Willy is changed by remembering them." (Carson 48) The lapses fall into two categories. The first consists of mainly happy memories Willy has of being with his sons in 1928 (when Biff is 13, Happy is 11, and the family car is the Chevy) and in 1932 (when Biff at 17 is a high school football star, Happy at 15 is content to share his brother's glory, and the Chevy has accumulated 82,000 miles). Embedded in these scenes of Willy confidently advising and praising his adoring sons are hints of Willy's flawed thinking and its early effect on both sons, especially Biff. In the second category of memory lapse Willy relives the rare occasion when Uncle Ben shows up for a brief visit. These scenes provide glimpses of their shared childhood and an older Willy, vulnerable and insecure, eager for advice and praise from Ben.

Willy informs us of the first time lapse in the play when he describes to Linda his confusion about which car he is driving. The first dramatized lapse occurs when he enters the kitchen at Linda's suggestion to make himself a sandwich with something called "whipped cheese." This lapse—signaled by a profusion of leaves that blocks out sight of the apartment buildings—is, according to Carson:

> . . . the result of his recollection of the time when Biff seemed so full of promise. It is brought on by Biff's return home and the inevitable tension between the two men which is the consequence of Biff's apparent inability to settle down. It begins with Willy remembering his son waxing the car and proceeds to recollections of other details such as the way in which Biff 'borrowed' a football. . . . The guilt Willy felt even then about exaggerating his own accomplishments and encouraging his sons to disregard the law is suggested by the appearance of Linda. . . . Since Willy could never deceive his wife with quite the same facility that he could impress his sons, Linda serves as a kind of conscience making him confess his true earnings and his real sense of inadequacy. . . . The temporary feeling of intimacy . . . reminds Willy that he has not even been honest with Linda, and he attempts to justify his infidelity . . . [but] the image of the woman . . . [reminds him that] in some ways, he has been more generous to his mistress than to his wife. (Carson 48–49)

Willy in these scenes is quick-tempered and impetuous, but he is not exhausted or defeated. High energy and feelings of hope and camaraderie dominate. For Willy in his present anguish, these relived episodes with youthful Biff and Happy bring a comforting happiness, but they also contain subtle signs of his desperation even back then and intimations that life will not turn out as he euphorically envisions it. These signs of impending trouble are easy for all to ignore at the time, because they are obscured by Willy's bravado and high hopes. Watching how and when these memories reassert themselves into his present mental state gives one the sense that Willy's subconscious mind is trying to get his attention not merely to bring comfort but to offer—if not solutions to the present crisis—some clues for understanding it.

We see, for example, in Willy's unlikely stories about having coffee with the mayor of Providence and boasting about receiving personal police protection for his car his deep-seated need for recognition and his inclination to exaggerate to the point of self-deception. As Carson has noted, even then he was overstating his earnings until gently coaxed to tell the truth by his patient and forgiving wife.

Similarly troubling is the display of what is now commonly referred to as "American exceptionalism"—the presumption of individual entitlement that permits those afflicted with this attitude to think they can ignore with impunity (and often do) established rules and customs. Willy rationalizes Biff's "borrowing" of the regulation football and apparently overlooks his driving without a license. Later, we see Willy praising his sons for stealing lumber from a nearby construction site. Willy proudly calls them "a couple of fearless characters," and Ben agrees, but realistic Charley warns, " . . . the jails are full of fearless characters."

Biff in these early scenes is in fact a promising young man, physically attractive and gifted with genuine athletic talent. At the same time, it is difficult not to fear that Willy's complacency about bending the rules and his insistence on Biff's special status ("If somebody else took that ball there'd be an uproar.") might produce in Biff an unrealistic—if not dangerously inflated—self-assessment. Biff must also endure his father's volatile moods, experiencing first his worshipful indulgence and then his angry eagerness to "whip" him into proper behavior. "Good behavior" for Biff includes doing well in school, but Bernard's tone of alarm about Biff's need to rely on his own work instead of cheating with Bernard's help or—Willy's solution—relying on his "very likable" personality, resonates with increasing legitimacy as the play proceeds. As these fragments of the past themselves move through time, they become darker and more explicitly ominous. It becomes clear that Willy suffered as a young man from mood swings and an almost unconscious and certainly bizarre habit of self-contradiction. He moves in a single fragment of conversation with Linda from an almost belligerent self-confidence ("Oh, I'll knock 'em dead next week. I'll go to Hartford. I'm very well liked in Hartford.") to a subdued admission of self-doubt ("You know, the trouble is, Linda, people don't seem to take to me."). Moments after joking about making jokes with prospective buyers, he describes an incident in which he imagined himself teased, to which he responded precipitously and, apparently, violently. If Willy actually "cracked" the offending person "right across the face," as he states, one wonders why he was not arrested for assault or fired. Accurate or not, the incident is an early sign of a highly unstable and vulnerable personality.

The episode ends with a more explosive manifestation of Willy's mental distress. He has just reaffirmed his love for Linda and his loneliness without her on the road when an unidentified woman's voice makes a disturbing intrusion into their confessional moment. Willy's guilt-ridden mind has summoned her. This jarring and instructive scene of Willy receiving reassurances about his prowess and appeal simultaneously from two women—one thanking him for stockings, the other having to mend her own torn pair—would not have been so memorably dramatized without Miller's innovative treatment of time and stage design.

Willy's Brief Interlude in the Present

Agitated and depleted by the emotional energy of his memories, Willy returns "wilting and staring" to the chronological present and finds himself with Happy, who has come down to the kitchen to rescue his father. Biff remains upstairs, immobilized by what he has heard. Happy's intervention consists mainly of glib reassurances that Willy rightly scorns as unrealistic. Later in the scene Happy will attempt to cheer his mother by announcing that he'll soon be getting married—a claim he is even less likely to follow up on than his promise to retire his father for life; and Linda, also realistic, knows it. "Go to bed, dear," she tells him. Happy is well-meaning (he has paid for Willy's respite in Florida) but thoroughly superficial in his response to life's contradictions and dilemmas. His easy answers bring on one of Willy's frightful outbursts: "The woods are burning!"

The guilt and sense of failure generated by this memory lapse prompt Willy into making protestations to Happy of his innocence ("I never . . . told him anything but decent things.") and excuses for his life. It is Willy's need for excuses that brings mention of Ben into the play: If only he had followed Ben's advice to get rich in Alaska! Willy describes Ben with clichés of American Dream rhetoric (". . . that man was success incarnate! . . . [He] knew what he wanted and went out and got it!"). Then, in this manic moment, he makes one of his curious comments, this one about not cracking open an oyster on a mattress. This gem of cautionary advice is almost certainly a platitude of the times (although it might be Willy's way of declaring that everyone besides himself and Ben, including Happy, is lazy). Either way, the comment illustrates Willy's "commonness," his fervent but unimaginative speech. It is certainly not a reference to himself; Willy is admirably hardworking.

Happy leaves as Charley, having overheard the commotion, walks in the door. Charley offers comfort, distraction, even a job (which prideful Willy rejects). Although scenes with Charley provide humorous diversions in the play, the banter between the two old friends exposes Charley's tolerant and placid nature and Willy's mercurial one. Willy is surprisingly combative and condescending with Charley. Beneath their genuine neighborliness is Willy's unacknowledged envy and anger toward a man like himself who has succeeded in the business world. But Charley lacks the energy and aspiration that animate Willy and attract audience sympathy to him.

Charley is content to not care, even suggesting that Willy treat his sons with a little benign forgetting. Willy's indignant and plaintive response ("Then what have I got to remember?") suggests both the impoverishment of his current life without the boys at home but also a certain generosity, a willingness to extend his paternal responsibility—even if guilt-driven—to accept the painful conditions of love and loss. These qualities in Willy contribute to his fatal anguish, but they are also appealing, even honorable. It is *his* life and death that break audience hearts, not Charley's.

Willy's Relived Memory with Ben
Willy's dismissal of Charley for not being a man "who can handle [his] tools" brings up a hallucinatory Ben who enters their conversation over cards. Briefly, Willy converses with both men until Charley, baffled and badgered, and too entangled in Willy's mental confusion, loses patience and departs in exasperation.

Without distractions, Willy now falls deeply into a second lapse which yields instructive insight about his earlier life. This remarkable memory reveals that Willy's family of origin was as dysfunctional as it was exciting. Uncle Ben—a "larger-than-life" figure with a blindfolded focus on having staggering amounts of wealth and power—apparently never included his brother's family on his extensive travel routes. Ben doesn't even know their mother has died (he calls her a "fine specimen of a lady") and neither son knows what became of their adventuring father beyond the day he walked out on all of them.

Ben's arrival sends Willy into a long reverie about his first years of life. In this recollection by a mind of its own memories, we learn that Ben and Willy were raised in the ethos of the frontier. This ethos is the mythical center of the American Dream. Lived with integrity and idealism, frontier life demanded physical courage, mental initiative, high spirits, and sustained resolve in order to survive. Ben recalls for Willy their inventive and romantic father: this "very great and very wild-hearted man . . . [would] start in Boston . . . toss the whole family into the wagon and drive the team right across the country. . . ." It is easy to speculate that these early happy associations with family trips likely influenced Willy's decision to become a traveling salesman. His references to opening up new territories ("[Before] I went north . . . the Wagner Company didn't know where New England was!") reinforce the idea that young Willy, imbued with the frontier spirit but also abandoned by a father more devoted to having his own adventures than to responsibly raising his family, may have chosen traveling (*not* selling) for a career to replicate a similar excitement and direction in his adult life but also to symbolically recover the lost father. Willy's excessive and impassioned involvement in his own sons makes more sense in this context, as does his tendency to be reckless about the law when it comes to finding building materials for his home. One recalls Willy's early enthusiasm for his car and trips to unfamiliar territories that made for exciting stories for his boys upon his return. But his actual journeys to New England were—by contrast and even at their best—only "wild-hearted" in a tawdry affair and have become, increasingly, occasions for frustration and failure.

Frontier life inspired the best in a person and also—notoriously—the worst. Willy seems not to have noticed the obvious signs of belligerence and corruption in Ben, no doubt because he is blinded by the way his brother has combined wealth with outdoor ruggedness and exotic travel. Ben's flaunting comments (which he repeats like a commercial for himself) about going into the jungle and emerging with so much dazzling wealth—he doesn't even keep accounts of it—never include any practical information about how he did it. (Years later, Willy and Happy are still wondering.) Interestingly, Ben is always in a hurry, as if fearful of something catching up to him.

Ben is an icon of success, the man who makes people believe those tales about pots of gold near rainbows and dollar bills growing on trees. Generations, including that of Willy's father, swarmed across the prairie searching for easy riches. But watching Ben's interactions with his nephews is instructive. Corruption is at the center of his bravado. Ben applauds the boys' not-so-petty theft of building supplies ("Nervy boy. Good!") and after challenging Biff to a fistfight knocks him ignominiously to the ground with the advice: "Never fight fair with a stranger, boy. You'll never get out of the jungle that way." Linda sensibly asks why Biff needs to be fighting at all; she is, in general, unimpressed by Ben, even resentful. By contrast, in Ben's presence, Willy becomes almost manic. He scornfully dismisses Linda's concerns. He brags to Ben that Biff is capable of chopping down the big trees whose actual destruction by the construction companies he will soon bitterly lament. And he gives a mixed message with the power to confuse and disable otherwise promising young men: He praises his sons for their "fearless" acts of theft and then "[gives] them hell" [for it].

Speculations about Willy in the Past and the Present

Did Willy half-believe his boys were frontiersmen so "special" and "fearless" as to be beyond the law? And with Ben's example and Willy's affirmation of it, did the boys grow up thinking they could get something for nothing, or, if not nothing, then with personal likeableness and Ben's questionable ethics? Has Willy confused his father's frontier spirit with the skills for success in the business world? These are not questions that Miller asks; they are questions that Miller imagines Willy's subconscious mind bringing to consciousness while he struggles mightily to keep disintegration and self-destruction at bay.

Willy's questions are—in important and still relevant ways—real questions for others besides Willy. Frontier life was alluring; Willy's father was appealing. He was adventuresome and hardworking. Also an inventor and artisan: With his own hands, he carved flutes that he sold to support the family. His success made possible a wandering lifestyle, one not bound by buildings or other people's schedules, one not like the life Biff bitterly characterizes as "a measly manner of existence." The flute music that accompanies Willy connects him with his father and is not ominous or oppressive. It is genuinely lyrical, innocent, and reassuringly simple, evocative of a different way of life. Perhaps Biff's inclination to whistle in elevators—that whimsical act ridiculed by Happy for being inappropriate behavior for anyone interested in "making it" in the business world—connects Biff unconsciously with his grandfather's flutes. Perhaps one explanation for the terrible tension between father and son is that they are more alike than different: animated by a similar spirit (originating for both in Willy's father) but choosing to follow separate and incompatible paths that lead each to frustration and despair. Clearly both have been profoundly affected by the loss of connection to the earth and open spaces. It is the tie that binds both to their lineage and national heritage. Are they animated by wrong ideas? Are their expectations outdated? Should they or anyone relinquish connection to the land in exchange for material success? Although the frontier was mostly gone by 1949, manifestations of national nostalgia for our pioneer past have always been ubiquitous.

By the end of Willy's memory of Ben's visit, it is clear that Ben has significance for Willy far more elemental than his aura of success. In Ben's presence, Willy is beside himself with fluctuating needs and emotions. Fatherless himself, Willy looks to his older brother for advice and confirmation while he ardently tries to impress him with his boys' manliness and half-true references to his own success. Ben's response is erratic and never helpful. He cavalierly praises the boys' antics but diminishes Willy with his condescension: "And good luck with your—what do you do?" Confronted by Willy's explicit request for more of his company, Ben imperiously responds: "I'll stop by on my way back to Africa." And to Willy's brave and revealing confession (" . . . I still feel kind of temporary about myself."), Ben can only come up with: "I'll be late for my train." Ben's visit is fundamentally unsatisfying and unproductive, yet Willy's need for him is both tenacious and inexhaustible.

Commenting on the instructive insights provided by Willy's lapses into the past, Benjamin Nelson makes two helpful points. He writes in *Arthur Miller: Portrait of a Playwright*, "This series of episodes, which centers on Willy and his sons, shows the father trying to substantiate his ecstatic belief in the success ideal [of the American Dream] by superimposing it upon his children." (Nelson 109) Later he sums up: "Ultimately each event dredged out of his past makes the same point about Willy Loman: his life is caught in an unresolvable dichotomy between fact and fancy. He is unable to separate his individuality from his conception of himself as a supersalesman because he cannot truly differentiate between the two." (Nelson 109–110) Such elementary incoherence about identity is a likely consequence of being abandoned by a mythical father. Ben cannot and will not satisfy this need for a father. In Neil Carson's words, "Willy's problems as a father are shown to be a direct result of his deprivation as a son, and it is part of the richness of *Death of a Salesman* that its perspective encompasses three generations." (Carson 50)

Conclusion of Act 1
In a 1995 interview for BBC radio, Miller described the average person's experience of living through the Depression. He used images that are relevant for anyone living at the outer edges of economic or emotional survival: " . . . [There] is a feeling at the back of the brain that the whole thing can sink at a moment's notice . . . everything else is ephemeral. It is going to blow away, except what a person is and what a relationship is." (Bigsby, ed. 1) In the concluding scene of act 1, Willy has returned to the chronological present. All four family members are under the same roof for what will be their last night as a whole family. For different reasons, Willy, Linda, and Biff—each one in isolation— are experiencing that "feeling at the back of the brain."

When Linda answers Biff's question about what to do about Willy's bizarre behavior—"Oh, my dear, you should do a lot of things, but there's nothing to do, so go to sleep"—we hear the exhaustion of her day-to-day effort to keep Willy together. When she says "I live from day to day"—we hear her dread that "the whole thing can sink at a moment's notice."

Thomas Porter describes Willy's state of mind in this way:

When [Willy] momentarily faces reality—his inability to drive to Boston, the mounting bills and the dwindling income—he has to flee to the past and to project the future. The salesman cannot abandon the myth [of success] without reducing himself to zero. Thus, he must hope. (Porter 137)

For Willy this means projecting his hope onto Biff. For Biff it means carrying the burden of Willy's hopes. To save his father Biff must take on a filial task that threatens his own survival and the reconciliation between father and son that both urgently need. Linda, at the edge of her strength, makes Biff's task explicit. In the tense scene with her sons when she discloses the evidence that Willy's "accidents" are suicide attempts, she tells Biff: " . . . I swear to God! Biff, his life is in your hands!" Beneath all fears and doubts is the need for right relationship with oneself and others: ". . . everything . . . is ephemeral . . . except what a person is and what a relationship is." With this view in mind, the play can be understood as a drama less about failing dreams and more about the importance of the ties that bind. This is the substance of Linda's famous "Attention must be paid" speech. Although addressed to her sons about their exhausted father, its language suggests a voice with more authority, as if it were a commandment being delivered authoritatively to a wider audience. Attention, it seems to be saying, must be paid to every person.

By the time Willy returns from his walk to see the stars, his sons have fully grasped the extremity of the family crisis. Linda's speech has worked. Biff and Happy have vowed to change their ways. For Biff it entails a radical change.

Biff's Crisis

Biff has come home because he is tormented by a need to understand himself, to know "what a person is." At 34, he is, in his own words, still "just . . . a boy," unable to marry or find satisfying work. By coming home to confront the past, Biff is following an ageless pattern. He knows the pervasive irresolution in his life is tied to his relationship with his father. Late in the play, during their tumultuous final encounter, Biff will furiously accuse his father of fostering a delusional sense of entitlement—an assumption that all doors will automatically open on his path to success: " . . . I never got anywhere because you blew me so full of hot air that I could never stand taking orders from anybody!"

Linda understands one aspect of Biff's dilemma ("Biff, a man is not a bird, to come and go with the springtime."), but she has no inkling of the secret he has been carrying for years about Willy's infidelity to her. The harm to Biff from carrying so virulent a secret is detected in his cynical dismissal of Happy's naïve assumptions and his sudden apprehension at the mention of "a woman." The nature of the secret precipitates an early fall from innocence for Biff; it was a transfiguring event with reverberating consequences. The fleeting eruption of "the woman" out of Willy's unconscious into his conscious memory just moments earlier is a sign of her importance to Willy for his story about himself and the tormenting guilt she continues to represent. The secret shared by Biff and Willy binds them in an emotional firestorm. In this context, Biff's offer to stay home, get a job, and support his parents is a painful sacrifice of a dutiful son, but it is a bizarre sacrifice—and almost doomed not to succeed—because Biff is an adult and has more appropriate tasks to perform. Making this commitment also provides Biff with a clear and urgent focus, a temporary way out of his own tormenting confusion. Nonetheless, Biff's gesture—however obviously it rises out of alarm and a misdirected effort at self-rescue—seems also to be motivated by a son's genuine love for his father.

The Family's Crisis

In his introduction to *Arthur Miller: A Collection of Critical Essays*, Robert W. Corrigan makes an interesting assessment of Miller and his main characters by applying the categories of human development put forward by Erik Erikson. Erikson (in *Identity and the Life Cycle*, 1959) describes eight stages of growth, each with a defining crisis. The crises of identity, generativity, and integrity are acutely relevant to Willy and Biff. Identity formation is the struggle of late adolescence and early adulthood; generativity follows in middle age at the peak of one's productivity in society; and integrity is the achievement of perspective and self-acceptance in old age. Corrigan points out that several of Miller's adult characters, including Willy, are still suffering with unresolved identity crises. He observes that the death of each of these characters was brought on by an absence of self-understanding:

> . . . this blindness is . . . due to their failure to have resolved the question of identity at an earlier and more appropriate time in life. Miller presents this crisis as a conflict between the uncomprehending self and a solid social or economic structure—family, the community, the system. The drama emerges either when the protagonist breaks his connection with society or when unexpected pressures reveal that such a connection has in fact never even existed. Miller sees the need for such a connection as absolute, and the failure to achieve and/or maintain it is bound to result in catastrophe. (Corrigan 2–3)

One recalls here Willy's remark about feeling "temporary" and his unreflective allegiance to incompatible ideas about how to live and succeed. The salesman's business ethic dictates behavior that would endanger life on the frontier; the qualifications for survival on the frontier would likely land a businessman in jail; and Willy's own confused notions about winning success by being "likeable" are insufficient for achieving success of any kind. Conducting a life according to ideals that work for separate and different paradigms has left Willy bewildered and profoundly unsatisfied with his life. One remedy for dealing with the complex challenges encountered in life is reflection followed by awareness leading to informed choices that constitute a productive and satisfying identity. But Willy belongs to a class and a profession that do not foster (and might even discourage) self-understanding. Deprived of a father and lacking incentives and capacity for self-awareness, Willy had multiple reasons—even before he entered the salesman's unpredictable world—to feel "temporary about [himself]." His identity confusion has persisted into his older age, creating instability for the whole family and catastrophe for him and Biff.

For years Willy has been looking at Biff as an extension of himself, the bearer of his hope for the future. His disordered thinking likely originated at the 1932 Ebbets Field game when he effectively stopped time at the moment Biff in his eyes arrived at the height of his youthful glory and was still exuding great promise. Willy felt himself implicated in Biff's glory; he remembers the crowd calling out the name "Loman, Loman, Loman!" His psychological need to stop time, at this juncture of Biff's life was not understood at the time nor was it ever acknowledged later in the family. Such a desperate act of hubris committed by one family member ineluctably affects the other members, though perhaps in less acute and more disguised ways. The impairment of family functioning and integrity—although its underlying causes are at this point in the play unacknowledged and unarticulated—has been of long duration. Linda has confused her wife and mother roles: She warns her 63-year-old husband to "be careful on the stairs" and appears to be turning all her anger on her sons. Certainly, Happy has not become a responsible adult. He admits to his own identity confusion ("I don't know what the hell I'm workin' for"), and his self-serving ethics are typical of one who suffers from deep insecurities. Linda calls him "a philandering bum," and he seems to be one reckless step away from being found out. Interestingly, Linda reveals nothing about her life other than her efforts to save Willy's.

As for Biff, this frozen-in-time version of himself transcends the need for identity formation. Even language cannot define him: He was, in Willy's enraptured words, "[like] a young god. Hercules . . . something like that." Now that Willy has endured the ignominious loss of what stature and identity he had achieved—". . . they [took] his salary away . . . he's been on straight commission"—he is, in Linda's words ". . . a beginner, an unknown," and his sense of deprivation has become life-threatening. Willy cannot rest until Biff has achieved something commensurate with the larger-than-life image he has imposed on his son. And Biff's crisis will remain acute until he discovers and affirms who he is that is not merely Willy's dream, and he will need Willy's confirmation that he has done so. A family closer to breakdown than the Loman family at the end of act 1 would be hard to imagine.

The final hours of family life depicted at the end of act 1 are dominated by emotional extremes—dread, rage, euphoria—and sudden reversals into their opposites. When Willy learns that Biff has agreed to ask his old boss Bill Oliver for help starting a business of his own, he erupts into euphoria unrestrained by any realistic considerations. One of these considerations is the fact that Biff was a mere shipping clerk for Oliver, not one of his salesmen, and he stole basketballs from the store. Again Willy exaggerates, his hopeful imagination racing ahead to unlikely outcomes. Of course Biff will go into sporting goods! Of course he will succeed because "[he knows] sporting goods better than Spaulding, for God's sake!" And he sees money in Biff's hand before Biff has seen Oliver. When reminded of this obvious fact, he instantly punctures all hopes and sinks into his familiar despondency. Within a matter of seconds Biff goes from hearing Willy's excessive praise to hearing his unjustified scorn: "Ah, you're counting your chickens again." We can assume that Biff has endured countless similar experiences of his father's mercurial nature. Happy—caught up in the family need for optimism—proposes a partnership with Biff—"The Loman Brothers"—which Willy instantly pronounces "a one-million-dollar idea!" Thomas Porter comments:

> This scene is generated out of the heart of myth. 'Loman Brothers' has, for Willy and the boys, the ring of personality and solidarity and achievement. It would not entail entering the impersonal arena of the office; the boys would be 'out playin' ball again.' With no regular hours to cramp their freedom and no fierce outside competition, there would be the 'old honor and comradeship.' Sportsmanship, clean living, economic freedom would blend in a million-dollar enterprise, the ideal life crowned with financial achievement. Only the glowing pair who ran to carry their father's valises and to

listen to his prideful predictions would consider such a scheme 'talking sense.' (Porter 140)

The family member likely to feel doubt at this precarious family juncture is Linda, and she has important reservations which—a bit diffidently—she tries to make known. But she has, in Benjamin Nelson's words, "helped build a doll's house around [Willy who] has been doing [the same thing] to Biff and Happy." (Nelson 112) Of course, she, too, wants to hope, and it makes sense that she chooses to tread lightly. In any case, Willy is under too much pressure from his relentless inner agenda to even notice her. Almost obsessively, he interrupts her and dismisses all her interventions except those that bring him immediate comfort. At this point in his disintegration he can only hear reassuring words, only bear to consider a single outcome. "I see great things for you kids," Willy declares, "I think your troubles are over." And his, as well. Willy is determined to see his boss the next morning to ask for the less strenuous job of non-traveling salesman. Act 1 concludes as each family member summons the resources and courage needed to make the next day work out as planned, and the family makes a collective effort to rescue itself and prevail.

Act 2

The second act contains two of the most painful scenes in Western literature. It is now morning. Although Willy has slept—ominously—"like a dead one," music "bright and gay" introduces the scene, setting up a parallel between the happy adventuring of Willy's original family and the hopeful ventures to the wilderness of the business world that Willy and Biff are undertaking today. The nostalgic spell cast by the shaving lotion fragrance left by the departing sons kindles in Willy and Linda a new level of high expectations. The father will confront his current boss and the son will visit his old boss—both hoping their separate encounters will yield the same result: a lifesaving hold on a new life. Willy is—characteristically—swept up by his "fast-track" optimism, but on this morning he outdoes himself with visions of moving with Linda to a "little place out in the country" with room for chickens and a garden. Matthew Roudané calls this Willy's "inability to observe his own emotional speed limits." (Bigsby, ed. 79)

Although hints of Linda's complicity with Willy's illusions have been heard earlier in her encouraging assurances that he is "doing fine" and "will do better next week," these remarks can also be understood as the normal support a wife would give a husband in discouraging times. This morning, however, she seems to have thrown out her reservations and joined the illusion. "Handsome" Biff, for example, "could be a—anything" dressed in his blue suit. When she announces that he'd left earlier in a hopeful mood and "couldn't wait to get downtown to see Oliver," we wonder if she is telling the truth or imagining this change of heart because that change is essential for her husband's survival. Biff did make a commitment to the family the night before, but only an hour earlier he had bitterly called "a measly manner of existence" the life he is now pursuing. Miller is also careful to note that Biff goes to sleep barely able to be in his father's presence. Everything that has happened in the past is still with them. Linda's mood, in fact, suddenly deflates when she learns that Biff, not Willy, has removed the rubber tube found near the gas-powered water heater.

An important function of this morning scene is to establish for the audience a sense of commonality with Willy. When Linda mentions the car and refrigerator bills, we ask: Who has not dealt with mortgages, time payments, and "grace periods?" Who has not been deluded by clever advertising? Who has not felt anger when machines and gadgets malfunction, when appliances break down before one is finished paying for them? Who has not felt "temporary" at some time or been fearful of not "making it?" When Willy says, "I'm always in a race with the junkyard!" he may be referring unconsciously to his own fate, but he is also speaking the truth for all of us. When he accuses manufacturers of "[timing] those things so when you finally [pay] for them, they're used up," we share his cynicism and it is justified. Miller was convinced that we all "knew Willy." At the deepest level all human beings need hope to keep going. Many people are animated by hopes that are as unlikely to come about as Willy's are. Willy's hopefulness is not why he fails. When he walks out the door on the way to see Howard, he carries expectations that are not unreasonable.

The Meeting with Howard

Willy's meeting with Howard is a pivotal scene in the play. Willy finds Howard in his office fiddling with a tape recorder, recently invented and typical of the mechanical gadgets that were quickly proliferating in the postwar economy. Howard is so mesmerized by the intricacies of his new possession that he does not notice that Willy is supposed to be on the road today. Nor is he aware of Willy's need or mission. For several minutes Willy functions as Howard's audience, an occasion to show off his children's voices that were awkwardly recorded the night before. Remembering that Willy and Linda count pennies to make their payments, it is uncomfortable to watch as he hears Howard's casual reference to the cost ("only a hundred and a half") and offhand assumption that every family has a maid at home to record favorite programs for later listening.

The outcome of the meeting is worse than Willy could have anticipated. Howard first declines to give Willy the job change he has requested and then takes away the job he has. To each effort Willy makes to plead his case—each one diminishing in size and dignity as he grows more desperate—Howard gives the infamous "yes, but" response and refers to him as "kid." His question to Willy—"But where am I going to put you, kid?"—recalls Linda's admonition to Biff earlier in the day: "Be loving to [your father]. Because he's only a little boat looking for a harbor." In all Willy hears eight "buts" in a 30-second conversation that concludes with Howard's remark: "Well, you gotta admit, business is business." Willy has no place, no safe harbor, no room for a garden, and now no job. In the economic system Willy belongs to, having no job is equivalent to having no identity.

The scene of Howard firing Willy created controversy for Miller. At one extreme is Eleanor Clark's commentary accusing Miller of creating an "intellectual muddle" by compromising ideology with attempts to make Willy's fate universally relevant. She writes:

It is, of course, the capitalist system that has done Willy in; the scene in which he is brutally fired after some forty years with the firm comes straight from the party-line literature of the thirties, and the idea emerges lucidly enough through all the confused motivations of the play that it is our particular form of money economy that has bred the absurdly false ideals of both father and sons. (Welland 52)

Raymond Williams in a passage cited earlier sees a system in which loyal participants like Willy slowly become commodities themselves, which in turn become outmoded and discarded. Some critics who praised the play for its ideology criticized Miller for not going far enough. Samuel Siller, writing in 1949 for *Masses & Mainstream*, felt Miller had undermined his own point by including a benign capitalist in the figure of Charley. And playwright Lorraine Hansberry sees Willy as emblematic of the irony at the center of the American dream:

a nation of great military strength, indescribable material wealth, and incredible mastery of the physical realm [is] unable . . . to produce a typical hero who [is] capable of an affirmative view of life. . . . Something has indeed gone wrong with at least past of the American Dream, and Willy Loman is the victim of the detour. (Hansberry 7)

Other critics point out that Willy's numerous personal flaws precipitate his own downfall. They cite evidence for Willy's moral laxity with his sons, his self-deceptions, his reactive personality, and, most directly relevant, his ineffectual efforts to make enough sales to justify ongoing service to the firm. Critic Arthur Gantz argues that Willy was simply a foolish man who wrongly believed that "success in the business world [could] be achieved not by work and ability but by being 'well-liked,' by a kind of hearty popularity that [would] open all doors and provide favors and preferential treatment." (Gantz 125–28) Gantz points out that after Howard reminds Willy that "business is business," Willy says he agrees but behaves as if he does not. Against Howard's objections, Willy offers a story about the legendary Dave Singleman which is subjectively—but not objectively—relevant, and Willy does not recognize the difference.

Paula Marantz Cohen takes an approach which makes considerations of ideology less relevant. In her essay "Why is Willy confused?" Cohen suggests reading *Death of a Salesman* with a focus on the paradigm shift beginning to take place at the historical time of the play. The transition from labor and machine productivity to intellectual and technical power restructures the methods of communication that organize a society. In this context she sees Willy's traveling salesman job as sharing the one-way extractive mentality of the pioneers: Set your goal, make your sales pitch, take what you can get, and move on. Interestingly, she sees Willy's style of selling through being a likeable and engaging personality more useful for an age when most people have discretionary money and are more likely to make purchase choices based on personal associations. She writes:

> Significantly, it is Howard who introduces the single symbol of the new in the play. . . . [The tape recorder] is a device that is mechanical without being productive in any obvious sense. It doesn't make anything but noise and, when not mobilized for communication purposes, it seems a childish indulgence. Yet the machine is meaningful in a historical context. It symbolizes the beginning of a new wave of communication devices for business use. . . . Miller provides us with a clue [to the machine's future usefulness] in the figure of Bernard, the play's representative of the future. Bernard is in the field of communication; he is a litigator, and his profession is destined to play a powerful role in the coming information society. . . . (Roudané, ed. 128)

Cohen speculates that the outcome in Howard's office might have been different had Willy asked, "Did your father ever tell you . . . ?" instead of "Your father came to me the day you were born. . . ." Delivered this way, the statement allows no room for a response. It is packaged sentiment and seems drawn out of the very salesman's kit that can no longer sell the buyers in New England. Willy ends up selling himself out of a job because his plea brings home to his employer, if only subliminally, the ineffectiveness of the old-style salesmanship with its reliance on one-way communication. (Roudané, ed. 128) She praises Miller for what she regards as his "intuitive grasp of the direction of his society's evolution." (126)

Critic Ronald Hayman does not comment directly on Willy's being fired but reminds us that the claustrophobia that Willy expresses when speaking of his home "is linked with the mechanization and urbanization [of his time] and [his] madness is linked with a nostalgia for the better times in the past." (Hayman 30) When Willy cannot control the tape recorder after Howard has left the room, he responds hysterically like one both mad and claustrophobic. Similarly, Matthew Roudané suggests that Willy's response to Howard's machine is "a symbolic reminder of how far Willy lags behind his own technological era. . . ."

> When [the machine] talks to Willy [he] has no idea of how to turn off the new-fangled invention. The taped voice of Howard's son spinning out of control foregrounds, of course, Willy's own life, which is spinning out of control. After all, Willy does not fit in with the industrialized world; he is more at home in a pastoral world, one in which he can use his hands to build a porch or plant seed in a garden. (Bigsby, ed. 76)

Critic Dennis Welland in his book on Miller reviews some of the differing interpretations of Howard's treatment of Willy and concludes: "The evidence for a Marxist interpretation of *Death of a Salesman* is . . . not very impressive. The scene [of Willy's firing] is theatrically . . . moving [and] painful . . . but it engenders a mixture of pity and exasperation rather than the indignation that we would expect of a 'party-line' literature. . . ." (Welland 54) Welland joins other critics in noting the presence of successful-but-also-kindly Charley as a contrast to Howard. Welland attributes Howard's dismissal of Willy to his self-absorption:

> The tape-recorder scene serves two purposes in the scene: when Willy . . . sets it accidentally in motion it precipitates a hysterical breakdown that symbolizes the central theme of the play in Willy's horror at his inability to switch it off—to switch off the recorded past. Whether the past is that of his own sons recorded on his memory and conscience, or that of Howard's son recorded on a mechanical instrument, it is the past, more than capitalism, of which Willy is always the victim. . . . The machine also [dramatizes] Howard's ingenuous pride in his children. They are far more real to him than is the memory of his father to which Willy constantly appeals, and his pride in their prowess and their affection for him obliterates any understanding of Willy's plight, exactly as Willy's pride in his sons has blinded him to any recognition of the worth of Bernard. (54)

Although artists do not control the range of meanings their works may reflect, Miller has been unusually accessible to his audiences, and it is always illuminating to hear him speak about his intentions. His comments about producing *Death of a Salesman* in China are especially useful because he was challenged to explain himself to actors unacquainted with American ideas. He had also been thinking about his most famous character for 34 years. Miller instructed the actor playing Howard: " . . . Willy is trying to tell you . . . that the impersonality of business is destroying him. . . . Your answer is that you are helpless to do anything for him, you are both caught in the same machine." (*"Salesman" in Beijing* 135) He then converses with the other actors about the transition in China from socialist theory that emphasizes cooperation between people to the recent commercialization of life where, increasingly, specialists are trained and paid for work that used to be done by the community. He concludes that the play "does not have the solution to this problem—the alienation brought by technological advance—because I don't have the solution. What I present is the price we pay for our progress." (136)

This acknowledgment brings criticism from Tom Driver, who accuses Miller of "[lacking] that metaphysical inquisitiveness which would have taken him to the bottom of the problems he encounters." He cites the "ambiguity . . . in the question of society versus the individual" and asks, "[Is the 'law' that Willy breaks] imposed upon him by a white collar industrial society? If so, what is wrong with such a society and what truth does it prevent Willy from seeing?" (Bloom 17)

Similarly, Eric Mottram praises Miller's evocation of the human suffering embodied in Willy but asks: ". . . if the hero dies at his own hand, with the sense of waste and bewilderment still entire within him, who can now be interested in anything but the chance of changing the . . . society that brings him to that degradation?" (Corrigan, ed. 32)

Arthur Miller had been interested in politics since his college years and active over the years in labor and other issues speaking out against injustices committed by corporations and governments (including his own). But he was an artist first:

> A play cannot be equated with a political philosophy. . . .
> I do not believe that any work of art can help but be
> diminished by its adherence at any cost to a political
> program, including its author's, and not for any other
> reason than that there is no political program—any more
> than there is a theory of tragedy—which can encompass
> the complexities of real life. Doubtless an author's politics
> must be one element, and even an important one, in the
> germination of his art, but if it is art he has created it must
> by definition bend itself to his observation rather than to
> his opinions or even his hopes. (*Collected Plays* 36)

Interlude with Ben

Irrespective of the role American capitalism played in Willy's fate, Willy himself responds to his mortification with a declaration and a story about his origins. Recalling the inspiration that propelled him into the selling business, he reminds Howard that back then "there was personality in it . . . there was respect, and comradeship, and gratitude in it. . . . [unlike] today [when] it's all cut and dried. . . ." With a minimum of ritual politeness Howard ushers Willy out the door, leaving him with the almost certain false promise that he'll reconsider if Willy goes home and takes a long rest. Failing to recover any stability or peace of mind with his visit to Howard, Willy departs and falls into another memory lapse with Ben. One imagines him here as Miller once described him—a normal-appearing man mumbling to himself—this time on a New York City sidewalk on his way, without quite knowing it, to Charley's office.

Willy is animated by images of mythical places. In his conversation with Howard, he evokes a plush and comforting image of the salesman's territory that ends with the inspiring funeral of Dave Singleman. Here his unconscious memory has summoned Ben from a mythical frontier, a mythical jungle, because he associates Ben with a pivotal choice he made in the past. Willy punishes himself by persistently wondering how his life would be different had he followed Ben to Alaska.

This episode—like Willy's other memory lapses—is not a reliable source of objective information, only of Willy's selective remembering. To the extent that he accurately recalls Linda in these scenes, we can discern that she had a more active and complex role in Willy's life than earlier scenes have suggested. Linda is not happy to see Ben on this, his second visit to the family. To Ben's alluring description of rugged work in his newly acquired timberland, Linda insists, "He's got a beautiful job here [and] is doing well enough. . . ." Ben's condescending answer—"Well enough for what?"—is a real question with much more than Willy's material success implied, although that consideration is in the playwright's mind (and ours), not Ben's. Was moving to Alaska a realistic option for the Loman family? Linda shows no potential for being a happy prairie woman or lumberjack's wife; she seems here to be protecting a stable and secure—if dull and unchallenging—way of life for herself and her family. It is easy to simplify Linda.

She is certainly loyal and lovingly supportive to her husband, but when he proclaims with determination, "We'll do it here, Ben," meaning staying in Brooklyn, has he allowed her to take away something vital in him? We recall that Willy was raised by his mother after his father deserted the family. Without paternal direction in his life, Willy may have become too accustomed to female influence. This scene may raise questions of blame, more interesting but perhaps less useful.

Willy's Meeting with Bernard and Charley

Willy arrives at Charley's office engaged out loud in a remembered conversation that took place on the day of the 1932 Ebbets Field game, in which he responds to Charley's teasing with inappropriate combativeness. We see Willy behaving like one "who can't take a joke," adding to the impression gained through earlier hints that he has difficulty with certain kinds of social interactions despite his insistence on being a likeable guy. Willy finds grown-up Bernard whistling to himself in his father's reception room. Clearly Happy is mistaken in his theory of the deleterious effects of whistling, because Bernard is stopping to visit his father on his way to argue a case before the Supreme Court. In Bernard's presence, Willy's inclination to exaggerate expands to the point of fantasy and his flawed reasoning leads to odd assumptions. He tells Bernard that Bill Oliver has summoned Biff from out west, and he is sure that people who have their own tennis courts must be "fine people" when they could just as easily be crooks. Nonetheless, the ensuing scene is the first in the play thus far in which respect, authenticity, and human decency dominate. Willy is gracious about Bernard's accomplishments; Bernard is self-effacing about those same accomplishments and genuinely solicitous with Willy; Charley, once again, offers Willy money, a job, and simple kindness; and Willy is finally truthful about himself and vulnerable with Charley.

This time Charley also gives Willy a clairvoyant and kindly message: "Willy, nobody's worth nothin' dead." There is something grimly inevitable about this chance meeting of Bernard, Charley, and Willy. Willy is a broken man now, clinging to his final hope that for his son Biff the day has gone well. He has arrived at the point in his mental disintegration where nothing remains to be lost and he can endure the most damaging and humiliating of his memories. The mystery is what motivates the return of these memories. Perhaps Willy has simply lost all his defenses. Perhaps the unconscious mind is a cruel tyrant. It is not possible to fathom the workings of the mind. But from this point on in the play—beneath the entire emotional conflagration still to come—there is something noble and certainly poignant in the sight of a despairing soul seeking explanations for his fate. To Bernard's counsel—". . . Sometimes, Willy, it is better for a man to just walk away"—Willy replies: "but if you can't walk away?" Miller sees in this incapacity to walk away one mark of a tragic stature. He writes about the moment of commitment in a play, "that moment when, in my eyes, a man differentiates himself from every other man, that moment when out of a sky full of stars he fixes on one star. I take it, as well . . . that the less capable a man is of walking away from the central conflict of the play, the closer he approaches a tragic existence." (*Collected Plays* 7)

"*Small and alone,*" Willy asks, "What's the secret?" Why did Bernard succeed and Biff fail? He recalls Bernard inquiring about what happened to Biff on his visit to Willy in Boston that seemed to have broken Biff's spirit. Willy makes a final effort to beat back the dreaded memory before leaving to meet his sons at the restaurant.

The Restaurant Scene

If *Death of a Salesman* had been performed for the past 150 years instead of 50, we would know Marx's view of the scene with Howard and Freud's view of the restaurant scene. Sexuality, betrayal, and the elemental conflict between father and son are all dramatized in this climactic scene. The meeting for dinner at the restaurant—anticipated by each participant as an event of family celebration and communion—is, in fact, an occasion for the enactment of love among family members, but love at its most convoluted and desperate.

Happy arrives first with an air suggesting that he has either forgotten the original purpose of the family dinner or is ready to abandon it in exchange for some tawdry fun with the girls. In every exchange with the waiter and the two girls, Happy exposes his vanity, superficiality, and self-promoting aggressiveness. Somehow it is fitting that he makes a point of ordering lobsters with big claws for a dinner no one ever eats. Some critics find this scene unlikely; certainly, it is extreme. In no other scene in the play are the effects of being what Biff will later call being "[blown] full of hot air" so plainly displayed. His flamboyant exaggerations ("Biff is quarterback for the New York Giants") and seductive salesman's talk create a deeply ironic setting for the arrival of Willy and Biff, who must disclose to each other the disastrous consequences these attributes may lead to.

Biff arrives next, ready to tell the truth, desperate to present to his brother and father, especially his father, an authentic version of himself, a story—however humiliating—he can tell with integrity. But Happy, whose stake in Biff's life was minimal until he concocted the "Loman Brothers" fantasy the night before, listens to the story but with less interest in its significance for Biff than in making sure Willy doesn't hear it. "[Tell] him something nice," is Happy's advice. He continues to think it's appropriate to try to fix Biff up with one of the random women in the restaurant. The brothers could not be less alike here. Happy has inherited his Uncle Ben's bravado and extractive mentality. Biff has inherited his grandfather's wanderlust, which he has been struggling to put into a form that will earn his father's approval. Earlier that morning, Biff had approached Oliver with the assumption that he would be remembered as a good salesman rather than the shipping clerk who stole a carton of basketballs. The moment when Oliver doesn't recognize Biff is the occasion for Biff to recognize himself for the first time.

At the center of Biff's epiphany is his impulsive theft of Oliver's pen. Superficially a reckless act, it may have served an important unconscious purpose—namely, rescuing Biff from ever having to work for Oliver or anyone like him. In the final confrontation between Biff and his father that occurs later in the evening, Biff describes himself leaving Oliver's office in a way that supports this interpretation:

> I ran down eleven flights with a pen in my hand today. And suddenly I stopped, you hear me? And in the middle of that office building, do you hear this? I stopped in the middle of that building and I saw—the sky. I saw the things I love in this world. The work and the food and the time to sit and smoke. And I looked at the pen and said to myself, what the hell am I grabbing this for? Why, am I trying to become what I don't want to be?

Paula Cohen discusses the issue of stealing in the context of family dynamics:

> Willy fails to see how lessons he has taught at home may take shape in other contexts. In the flashback scenes, Willy thus praises Biff for his initiative in stealing a football and in taking lumber from a nearby site to rebuild the front stoop; later, when an adult Biff confesses to his father that he stole Bill Oliver's pen, Willy will not hear the confession. We see that Biff has become a thief because of the messages he received at home and that home, which should be a source of comfort and forgiveness, is precisely the place where his confession can not be heard. (Roudané, ed. 129)

Matthew Roudané expands the notion of theft:

> From Happy's stealing other executives' fiancées to Biff's stealing the high school football, the box full of basketballs, the lumber and cement from the neighborhood, the suit in Kansas City, and Bill Oliver's fountain pen, the question of stealing deepens to encompass not only social crimes but fundamental issues, private issues: the stealing of one's very identity, the loss of the self, the abrogation of responsibility. (Bigsby, ed. 69)

Roudané's view is consistent with the charge against capitalism to the extent that the commercialization of culture robs individuals of their inner nature. It is the sensation of recovering one's inner nature that Biff experiences with Oliver. And the emotional release that follows such a hard-earned moment of truth energizes Biff's behavior in the restaurant. He is ready to be his own man, but neither his brother nor his father will permit it. Biff and Willy have parallel stories to bring to the restaurant, but for several moments after Willy's arrival, each can only concentrate on the other's failure. Biff is stunned to learn that Willy has been fired, while Willy attempts to reinvent Biff's story according to the optimistic expectations he has been carrying around all day. Biff, who is newly determined to "hold on to the facts tonight," finds Willy's distortions—and Happy's complicity in them—unbearable, and he seems ready to flee in exasperation rather than stay and join the old family pattern of fixing things by mutual and multiple deceptions. Only after Biff panics at the sight of Willy spinning out of control, frantic with guilt and pain, does he succumb to Happy's advice. "Pop, listen!" he beseeches, "Listen to me! I'm telling you something good," and then he lies about Oliver responding to their "Loman Brothers" scheme.

Biff cannot sustain this deception. The truth comes out anyway, and Willy is utterly undone by it. He is seized by the memory of hiding his mistress in the hotel washroom. Staggering out of his chair, Willy stumbles toward the restaurant restroom, where he sinks into a reenactment of his most dreaded memory: Biff's discovery of his infidelity to Linda. Remarkably, Happy is mainly concerned here with restoring the impression he had earlier made on Miss Forsythe, who has gone off to fetch a date for Biff. Happy is misguided in his priorities, while Biff, who needs to flee from this terrible scene, takes a stand before he leaves. Resentful of the inappropriate intrusion of Happy's women into a critical and plainly private family episode, Biff announces with great feeling: "Miss Forsythe, you've just seen a prince walk by. A fine troubled prince. A hardworking, unappreciated prince. A pal, you understand? A good companion. Always for his boys." A moment later, Happy will betray this "prince [who was] always for his boys" by denying that Willy is his father. "He's just a guy," he tells the women as they depart together, abandoning Willy in the restroom.

The Woman

While Biff is telling the world, in effect, that his father is a "prince," Willy is in the throes of his nightmarish memory in which this same son called him "[A] fake! [A] phony little fake!" Biff's discovery of his father's infidelity takes place in the summer of 1932—a few months after his victorious game at Ebbets Field. Within a year Biff provides his father with his moment of greatest glory and moment of greatest shame. Despite Bernard's help, Biff has failed math by four points and won't be able to attend college as planned. Knowing he can count on his father, Biff makes a surprise trip to Boston, where Willy is on a sales trip. Biff's discovery of Willy's mistress in his hotel room—his witness to a perversion of the primal scene—reminds critic Leonard Moss of the ancient family drama involving what Shakespeare in *King Lear* called 'unnaturalness between child and the parent'—'the bond crack'd 'twixt son and father':

> *Death of a Salesman* . . . repeats that archetypal plot in which a son . . . looks to his father for moral direction . . . instead finds corruption . . . and severs the bond of mutual respect. . . . [This] breach of trust, shame and resentment prevent permanent reunion. . . . Biff . . . suffers an emotional and moral shock experienced by numerous other literary figures, including the biblical Adam. . . . He begins in security and innocence; proceeds through enlightenment, indignation, disillusion, and despair; and ends in cynical, sorrowful resignation. (Moss 24–25)

Matthew Roudané focuses on Willy in this scene:

> Miller fills the daydream scene in Boston with images of a fall, moving from the chair at Frank's Chop House to the bed in the Standish Arms [where Willy has fallen into bed with The Woman]. . . . After hearing Biff's knocking on the

door, she pleads , 'Willy, . . . are you going to get up, get up, get up, get up?' while the audience watches a man in the process of falling down, down, down, down. (Bigsby, ed. 67)

In this scene Miller makes Biff's struggle equal to Willy's struggle. How is a son to behave when the father he admires and is ready to emulate has also been the occasion for irrevocable disillusionment? Biff, weeping, crumbles before Willy after Willy has banished the character referred to as The Woman from the room. Willy responds with two voices: "She's nothing to me, Biff. I was lonely. . . ."; and, seconds later, when Biff, unable to accept his explanation, tries to leave, not reconciled, Willy aggressively asserts his authority: "I gave you an order." Biff does not obey and leaves Willy alone on the hotel room floor, as he and Happy have just left him alone in the restaurant. We don't see Biff in the months and years that follow this encounter, but we do see the consequences. In the conversation Willy has with Bernard in Charley's office, we learn that Biff disappeared for a month after his trip to Boston, and when he returned, he burned his college sneakers, fought with Bernard, and refused to go to summer school where he could have made up the lost credit. "I've often thought," says Bernard, "of how strange it was that I knew he'd given up his life." And then the question that pierces Willy's heart: "What happened in Boston, Willy?" Since the play gives no clues to the contrary, we can assume that Biff has been carrying his secret alone all these years. In family dynamic terms it would be labeled a "toxic secret," and much evidence could be produced showing the virulent effect on the secret bearer and the insidious effect on the others involved. We do know that in recent years Biff has been unsettled (like "a bird . . . [coming] and [going] with the springtime"), and we are soon to learn that he's been in jail for a series of petty thefts. It is impossible not to wonder how different Biff's life might have been had Willy had the courage to acknowledge the secret. Willy's life might have been different as well. But Miller's play is not about hindsight. The irony is that Biff knows too much about his father, who in turn knows too little about his own son.

Miller writes, "The assumption—or presumption—behind [my] plays is that life has meaning." (*Collected Plays* 8) Heading home alone from the restaurant, Willy makes meaning by choosing between two ideals that he cannot make compatible: He gives away his money and goes in search of seeds. "Nothing is planted," he tells Stanley, who at this moment is standing in for anyone paying attention. "I don't have a thing in the ground." Father and sons come home—separately—and conclude their aborted conversation begun in the restaurant. For Willy and Biff it is the final occasion to end the sound and fury between them and redeem the meaning of their relationship. Biff finds Willy in the garden in a scene that reminds critic Ronald Hayman of Shakespeare:

> One scene which demands powerful language is the late-night seed-planting scene. . . . Finally aware that he has ignored too long the call of the open air, Willy pathetically tries to plant seeds by torchlight. Had the dialogue been weakly written, this scene would merely have made him look ludicrous. Instead, madly talking to his dead brother, he is almost like a salesman-Lear on a garden/heath. The poetry spreads from the action to the language, which is simple, unpretentious, innocent of any rhetorical inflation, but pregnant, specific, and thoroughly effective. (Hayman 36)

Some readers are inclined to dismiss Willy's ravings in his "garden" as psychotic, but Miller insists that we must not. Lamenting the "decision to play Willy as a psycho" in the Stanley Kramer film version of the play, Miller wrote:

> As a psychotic, he was predictable in the extreme; more than that, the misconception melted the tension between a man and his society. . . . If he was nuts, he could hardly stand as a comment on anything. (*Timebends* 315)

As Willy goes about measuring seed rows, he tells the ghost of Ben: "A man can't go out the way he came in, Ben, a man has got to add up to something." This is not a psychotic statement. Miller cited in his vision of the play "the image of a need greater than hunger or thirst, a need to leave a thumbprint somewhere on the world . . . [even knowing that in doing so] one has carefully inscribed one's name on a cake of ice on a hot July day." (*Collected Plays* 29) In Willy's pain-wracked thinking, he is planting (leaving a literal thumbprint on the earth) metaphorical seeds because his favored son has—under values he's symbolically abandoned in the restaurant—come to nothing.

Willy is planting a garden in an industrial landscape. It is obvious to link him here with Adam in—or being banished from—the first garden. Also easy to reject as a sentimental, pastoral illusion is any notion of going back to a simpler life, of recovering the frontier, of making once again a connection to the land a central experience and value. But Miller has dramatized here some of the real consequences of living in a mechanized society and, as he stated in *"Salesman" in Beijing* and elsewhere, knows something inestimable and essential has been lost. Willy wants to open windows that are already open. What would he do in a contemporary building with windows that cannot be opened? Many people are drawn to Willy because he protests the loss of a beloved way of life and will not give up hope. Although Willy's failings undermine his chance for happiness, is it not possible to see in his final act of planting seeds a warning—along with all the sad, crazy confusion—too late for him but not for his audience, that we have collectively made a profound error about the values we live by?

Somewhere in the garden Willy falls irrevocably into the plan to end his life. With the help of Ben's ghost, Willy ponders the question of suicide as a cowardly act but settles it with another question: "Does it take more guts to stand here the rest of my life ringing up zero?" In Ben's presence Willy imagines death as a kind of pioneering journey into the dark wilderness where his insurance money will turns into diamonds and both his and Biff's life are redeemed. Of course Willy's thinking is fraught with confusion: It is a spiritual redemption gained through making himself a commodity; insurance companies may not pay for suicidal death; Biff needs Willy's honesty and unconditional love more than he needs his money; and, what happens to Linda? Miller raises these issues quite plainly but appears to care more about the final moment of confrontation between Willy and Biff, in which both are transfigured.

Raymond Williams writes, "The persuasive atmosphere of the play . . . is one of false consciousness—the conditioned attitudes in which Loman trains his sons—being broken into by real consciousness, in actual life and relationships." (Corrigan, ed. 7) Biff has come home to tell the truth and, in doing so, to make himself free. Willy needs confirmation that he isn't "[going] out the way he came in, [that he does in fact] add up to something." When Biff furiously yells, "We never told the truth for ten minutes in this house!" he has broken through the false consciousness that afflicts the family. And when Willy responds to Biff's self-acknowledgement—"Pop! I'm a dime a dozen and so are you!"—he is confirming that he is not "[going] out the way he came in." Roudané writes:

> Willy Loman's real condition lies in his insecurity in the universe, his profound sense of being unfulfilled. . . . No question Willy exaggerates, cheats, and lies, charges which he is ill equipped to refute but well suited to deny. But when he screams to Biff, 'I am not a dime a dozen! I am Willy Loman, and you are Biff Loman!" . . . is he not laying claim, not only to his dignity and individual worth but also to every person's worthiness? (Bigsby, ed. 79)

This is not a perfect moment. Happy immediately tries to undo Biff's statement by insisting the family never lies—which is a lie in itself. And in the Requiem, Happy shows no sign of change or insight. He vows to continue in his father's career path, perhaps more aggressively, as if to show "them" who the Loman men really are. But Biff will not follow in Willy's path. What Biff *will* do is unclear. He asks Willy to "let [him] go," and in the broken-down rush of tears that comes as he holds on to Willy, the kind of love that permits this release finally flows between them. Miller called Willy's recognition of Biff's love an "epiphany." Describing a late rehearsal in China, Miller observes that his Willy-actor:

> has ceased to feel he is empty in the final confrontation scene with Biff, for the same reason none of us feels empty when love is in us. Willy is a lover forsaken and seeking a lost state of grace, and the great lift of the play is his discovery, in the unlikeliest moments of threats and conflict, that he is loved by his boy, his heart of hearts. (*"Salesman" in Beijing* 247)

The Requiem

Each of those at the grave site responds characteristically. Practical Charley, probably unable to bear too much emotion, worries about the darkening day. Happy, speaking with his father's bizarrely combative style, takes Willy's death as a personal affront and nearly assaults Biff for speaking the truth. Biff is indirectly revealing his true self when he speaks the truth about his father; he is solicitous of his mother and knows about dreams. Linda has spent so much time protecting Willy from himself that she seems not to have understood his dreams, and now she does not understand what has befallen her. She is grief-stricken to find herself "free and clear" without him. Nearly mute with sorrow, and probably remembering Willy's story about Dave Singleman's famous funeral, she asks, "Why didn't anybody come?" Her love for her husband is almost palpable. Self-effacing Bernard stays in the background.

Some new and unexpected events occur in the Requiem. Charley, whose sentences are always plain—even (like Willy's) cliché-ridden—suddenly becomes lyrical. Speaking as Miller might or possibly stirred by Biff's insight and a need to intervene against Happy's aggressiveness, Charley likens a salesman's condition to that of a lonely wanderer, not unlike that of a pioneer—being "way out there in the blue." Earlier he had reminded Willy that the " . . . only thing you got in this world is what you can sell." Charley reminds us now that, in the culture of selling, "No man only needs a little salary." And any man would feel "kind of temporary about [himself]." Biff, too, is different. Released now, by the truth-telling encounter with his father, to accept himself, Biff can remember and speak about what was good in his past. Released also from the frozen moment in Willy's mind where he was imprisoned by his father's self-serving adoration, Biff has recovered his history and this must happen before he can recover his life.

These insights and developments are the stuff of tragedy, but not of the classical kind. Miller was not concerned about this distinction, but many critics were and are. Their conflicting views and reflections are found abundantly in the extensive commentary generated by Miller's work. A range of opinion exists about Willy Loman. To Mary McCarthy, Willy is a "cut-out figure . . ." typical of those inhabiting the American advertiser's view of American life. (McCarthy xv) Robert Hogan calls Willy a character of "rare meaningfulness." (Hogan 20) Benjamin Nelson writes:

> Willy Loman is intrinsically American, but in his particularity he also attains universality. Shot through with weaknesses and faults, he is almost a personification of self-delusion and waste, the apotheosis of the modern man in an age too vast, demanding and complex for him. But without abrogating his intense individuality, he is also the archetypal father, not far removed in his hopes, mistakes, catastrophe, and reconciliation from that most ludicrous and sublime of all archetypal parents, King Lear. Finally, he personifies the human being's desire, for all his flaws, to force apart the steel pincers of necessity and partake of magnificence, and in this need he becomes a profoundly relevant man for all ages. (Nelson 134)

Willy has had a powerful effect on many audiences; people respond to him as if he were a real person. Miller tells a story about a famous retail magnate who was so affected by the play that at its conclusion he walked up to the front of the theater to publicly announce that no employee in his firm would ever be fired because of his age. (*Timebends* 191) Miller also recalls the feelings he had while writing the play in some little outbuilding on his Connecticut homestead: "Stepping out the door exhausted at the end of a day [I looked] up at the night sky and said 'Talk to me, Willy, what should I say?' He seemed to be there in the woods, watching me through the leaves, standing there in his pleated trousers, felt hat, with the valises in the weeds." (*"Salesman" in Beijing* 251)

Works Cited

Bigsby, Christopher, ed. *Arthur Miller and Company*, London: Methuen Drama in association with the Arthur Miller Centre for American Studies, 1990.

————, ed. *Cambridge Companion to Arthur Miller*. New York: Cambridge University Press, 1997.

Brater, Enoch, "Miller's Realism and Death of a Salesman." *AM (20th Century Views): New Perspectives*. Ed. Robert A. Martin. Englewood Cliffs: Prentice Hall, 1982.

Carson, Neil. *Arthur Miller*. New York: St. Martin's Press, 1988.

Corrigan, Robert W., ed. *Arthur Miller: A Collection of Critical Essays*. Englewood Cliffs: Prentice Hall, 1969.

Driver, Tom. "Strengths and Weaknesses in Arthur Miller," *Tulane Drama Review* 4, May 1960.

Gantz, Arthur. *Realms of the Self: Variations on a Theme in Modern Drama*. New York: New York University Press, 1980.

Hansberry, Lorraine. "An Author's Reflections: Willy Loman, Walter Younger, and He Who Must Live," *Village Voice*, August 12, 1959, p. 7.

Hayman, Ronald. *Contemporary Playwrights: Arthur Miller*. London: Heineman Educational, 1970.

Hogan, Robert. *Arthur Miller*. Minneapolis: University of Minnesota Press, 1964.

McCarthy, Mary. *Sights and Spectacles*. New York: Farrar, Straus and Cudahy, 1956.

Miller, Arthur. *Collected Plays*. New York: Viking Press, 1981.

————. *"Salesman" in Beijing*. New York: Viking Press, 1984.

————. *Timebends*. New York: Grove Press, 1987.

Nelson, Benjamin. *Arthur Miller: Portrait of a Playwright*. London: Owen, 1970.

Porter, Thomas E. *Myth and Modern American Drama*. Detroit: Wayne State University Press, 1969.

Roudané, Matthew C. ed. *Approaches to Teaching Arthur Miller's "Death of a Salesman."* New York: Modern Language Association of America, 1995.

Rowe, Kenneth Thorpe. *A Theatre in Your Head*. New York: Funk & Wagnalls, 1964.

Critical Views

Returning to New York, . . . I turned to Willy Loman, a salesman always full of words, and better yet, a man who could never cease trying, like Adam, to name himself and the world's wonders. I had known all along that this play could not be encompassed by conventional realism, and for one integral reason: in Willy the past was as alive as what was happening at the moment, sometimes even crashing in to completely overwhelm his mind. I wanted precisely the same fluidity in the form, and now it was clear to me that this must be primarily verbal. The language would of course have to be recognizably his to begin with, but it seemed possible now to infiltrate it with a kind of superconsciousness. The play, after all, involved the attempts of his sons and his wife and Willy himself to understand what was killing him. And to understand meant to lift the experience into emergency speech of an unashamedly open kind rather than to proceed by the crabbed dramatic hints and pretexts of the "natural." If the structure had to mirror the psychology as directly as could be done, it was still a psychology hammered into its strange shape by society, the business life Willy had lived and believed in. The play could reflect what I had always sensed as the unbroken tissue that was man and society, a single unit rather than two. . . .

"It's all right. I came back" rolled over and over in my head. . . . I had skipped a few areas that I knew would give me no trouble in the writing and gone for the parts that had to be muscled into position. By the next morning I had done the first half, the first act of two. When I lay down to sleep I realized I had been weeping—my eyes still burned and my throat was sore from talking it all out and shouting and laughing. I would be stiff when I woke, aching as if I had played four hours of football or tennis and now had to face the start of another game. It would take some six more weeks to complete Act II.

My laughter during the writing came mostly at Willy's contradicting himself so errantly, and out of the laughter the title came one afternoon. *Death Comes for the Archbishop*, the *Death and the Maiden* Quartet—always austere and elevated was death in titles. Now it would be claimed by a joker, a bleeding mass of contradictions, a clown, and there was something funny about that, something like a thumb in the eye, too. Yes, and in some far corner of my mind possibly something political; there was the smell in the air of a new American Empire in the making, if only because, as I had witnessed, Europe was dying or dead, and I wanted to set before the new captains and the so smugly confident kings the corpse of a believer. On the play's opening night a woman who shall not be named was outraged, calling it "a time bomb under American capitalism"; I hoped it was, or at least under the bullshit of capitalism, this pseudo life that thought to touch the clouds by standing on top of a refrigerator, waving a paid-up mortgage at the moon, victorious at last.

But some thirty-five years later, the Chinese reaction to my Beijing production of *Salesman* would confirm what had become more and more obvious over the decades in the play's hundreds of productions throughout the world: Willy was representative everywhere, in every kind of system, of ourselves in this time. The Chinese might disapprove of his lies and his self-deluding exaggerations as well as his immorality with women, but they certainly saw themselves in him. And it was not simply as a type but because of what he wanted. Which was to excel, to win out over anonymity and meaninglessness, to love and be loved, and above all, perhaps, to *count*. When he roared out, "I am not a dime a dozen! *I am Willy Loman, and you are Biff Loman!*" it came as a nearly revolutionary declaration after what was now thirty-four years of leveling. (The play was the same age as the Chinese revolution.) I did not know in 1948 in Connecticut that I was sending a message of resurgent individualism to the China of 1983—especially when the revolution had signified, it seemed at the time, the long-awaited rule of reason and the historic ending of chaotic egocentricity and selfish aggrandizement. Ah, yes. I had not reckoned on a young Chinese student saying to a CBS interviewer in the theatre lobby, "We are moved by it because we also want to be number one, and to be rich and successful." What else is this but human unpredictability, which goes on escaping the nets of unfreedom? I did not move far from the phone for two days after sending the script to [Elia] Kazan. By the end of the second silent day I would have accepted his calling to tell me that it was a scrambled egg, an impenetrable, unstageable piece of wreckage. And his tone when he finally did call was alarmingly somber. "I've read your play." He sounded at a loss as to how to give me the bad news. "My God, it's so sad." "It's supposed to be." "I just put it down. I don't know what to say. My father . . ." He broke off, the first of a great many men—and women—who would tell me that Willy was their father. I still thought he was letting me down easy. "It's a great play, Artie. I want to do it in the fall or winter. I'll start thinking about casting." He was talking as though someone we both knew had just died, and it filled me with happiness. Such is art. . . .

[As] rehearsals proceeded in the small, periodically abandoned theatre on the ratty roof of the New Amsterdam on Forty-second Street, . . . [actor] Lee [J. Cobb] seemed to move about in a buffalo's stupefied trance, muttering his lines, plodding with deathly slowness from position to position, and behaving like a man who had been punched in the head. "He's just learning it," Kazan shakily reassured me after three or four days. I waited as a week went by, and then ten days, and all that was emerging from Lee Cobb's throat was a bumpy hum. The other actors were nearing performance levels, but when they had to get a response from Lee all their rhythms slowed to near collapse. Kazan was no longer so sure and kept huddling with Lee, trying to pump him up. Nor did Lee offer any explanation, and I wondered whether he thought to actually play the part like a man with a foot in the grave. . . .

On about the twelfth day, . . . Lee stood up as usual from the bedroom chair and turned to Mildred Dunnock and bawled, "No, there's more people now. . . . There's more people!" and, gesturing toward the empty upstage where the window was supposed to be, caused a block of apartment houses to spring up in my brain, and the air became sour with the smell of kitchens where once there had been only the odors of earth, and he began to move frighteningly, with such ominous reality that my chest felt pressed down by an immense weight. After the scene had gone on for a few minutes, I glanced around to see if the others had my reaction. Jim Proctor had his head bent into his hands and was weeping, Eddie Kook was looking shocked, almost appalled, and tears were pouring over his cheeks, and Kazan behind me was grinning like a fiend, gripping his temples with both hands, and we knew we had it— there was an unmistakable wave of life moving across the air of the empty theatre, a wave of Willy's pain and protest. I began to weep myself at some point that was not particularly sad, but it was as much, I think, out of pride in our art, in Lee's magical capacity to imagine, to collect within himself every mote of life since Genesis and to let it pour forth. He stood up there like a giant moving the Rocky Mountains into position. . . .

The whole production was, I think, unusual for the openness with which every artist involved sought out his truths. It was all a daily, almost moment-to-moment testing of ideas. There was much about the play that had never been done before, and this gave an uncustomary excitement to our discussions about what would or would not be understood by an audience. The setting I had envisioned was three bare platforms and only the minimum necessary furniture for a kitchen and two bedrooms, with the Boston hotel room as well as Howard's office to be played in open space. Jo Mielziner took those platforms and designed an environment around them that was romantic and dreamlike yet at the same time lower-middle-class. His set, in a word, was an emblem of Willy's intense longing for the promises of the past, with which indeed the present state of his mind is always conflicting, and it was thus both a lyrical design and a dramatic one. The only notable mistake in his early concept was to put the gas hot-water heater in the middle of the kitchen, a symbol of menace that I thought obvious and Kazan finally eliminated as a hazard to his staging. . . .

My one scary hour came with the climactic restaurant fight between Willy and the boys, when it all threatened to come apart. I had written a scene in which Biff resolves to tell Willy that the former boss from whom Biff had planned to borrow money to start a business has refused to so much as see him and does not even remember his working for the firm years ago. But on meeting his brother and father in the restaurant, he realizes that Willy's psychological stress will not permit the whole catastrophic truth to be told, and he begins to trim the bad news. From moment to moment the scene as originally written had so many shadings of veracity that Arthur Kennedy, a very intelligent citizen indeed, had trouble shifting from a truth to a half-truth to a fragment of truth and back to the whole truth, all of it expressed in quickly delivered, very short lines. The three actors, with Kazan standing beside them, must have repeated the scene through a whole working day, and it still wobbled. "I don't see how we can make it happen," Kazan said as we left the theatre that evening. "Maybe you ought to try simplifying it for them." I went home and worked through the night and brought in a new scene, which played much better and became the scene as finally performed.

The other changes were very small and a pleasure to make because they involved adding lines rather than cutting or rewriting. In Act I, Willy is alone in the kitchen muttering to himself, and as his memories overtake him the lighting brightens, the exterior of the house becomes covered with leaf shadows as of old, and in a moment the boys are calling to him in their youthful voices, entering the stage as they were in their teens. There was not sufficient time, however, for them to descend from their beds in the dark on the specially designed elevators and finish stripping out of their pajamas into sweaters and trousers and sneakers, so I had to add time to Willy's monologue. But that was easy since he loved talking to himself about his boys and his vision of them. . . .

Salesman had its first public performance at the Locust Street Theatre in Philadelphia. Across the street the Philadelphia Orchestra was playing Beethoven's Seventh Symphony that afternoon, and Kazan thought Cobb ought to hear some of it, wanting, I suppose, to prime the great hulk on whom all our hopes depended. The three of us were in a conspiracy to make absolutely every moment of every scene cohere to what preceded and followed it; we were now aware that Willy's part was among the longest in dramatic literature, and Lee was showing signs of wearying. We sat on either side of him in a box, inviting him, as it were, to drink of the heroism of that music, to fling himself into his role tonight without holding back. We thought of ourselves, still, as a kind of continuation of a long and undying past.

As sometimes happened later on during the run, there was no applause at the final curtain of the first performance. Strange things began to go on in the audience. With the curtain down, some people stood to put their coats on and then sat again, some, especially men, were bent forward covering their faces, and others were openly weeping. People crossed the theatre to stand quietly talking with one another. It seemed forever before someone remembered to applaud, and then there was no end to it. I was standing at the back and saw a distinguished-looking elderly man being led up the aisle; he was talking excitedly into the ear of what seemed to be his male secretary or assistant. This, I learned, was Bernard Gimbel, head of the department store chain, who that night gave an order that no one in his stores was to be fired for being overage. . . .

[After the play,] edging my way onto the stage, where I hoped to find a place to sit and rest, I saw as in a glorious dream of reward and high success three waiters in rich crimson Louis Sherry jackets arranging plates and silver on an extraordinarily long banquet table stretching almost the entire stage width. On its white linen tablecloth were great silver tureens and platters of beef, fowl, and seafood along with ice-filled buckets of champagne. Whose idea could this have been? What a glorious climax to the triumphant evening! Anticipating the heady shock of cold champagne, I reached for a gleaming glass, when one of the waiters approached me and with polite firmness informed me that the dinner had been ordered by Mr. Dowling for a private party. Robert Dowling, whose City Investing Company owned the Morosco along with other Broadway theatres, was a jovial fellow turning sixty who had swum around Manhattan Island, a feat he seemed to memorialize by standing straight with his chest expanded. I liked his childishness and his enthusiasms. I said that Mr. Dowling would surely not begrudge the play's author a well-earned glass of wine in advance of the celebration, but the waiter, obviously on orders, was adamant. I was dumbfounded, it must be somebody's joke, but a bit later, as Mary and I were leaving with the cast and their friends, we all stopped for a moment at the back of the theatre to watch with half-hysterical incredulity as this rather decorous celebratory dinner proceeded literally inside Willy Loman's dun-colored Brooklyn house, the ladies in elaborate evening gowns, the men in dinner jackets, the waiters moving back and forth with the food under a polite hum of conversation suitable for the Pierre Hotel dining room, and the diners of course totally oblivious to the crowd of us looking on laughing and cracking jokes. It reminded me of scenes from Soviet movies of the last insensible days of the czarist court. Dowling, an otherwise generous fellow, was simply exercising the charming insensitivity of the proprietor, something Broadway would begin to see more and more of, but never perhaps on so grandly elegant and absurd a scale.

Secretly, of course, I was outraged, but sufficient praise was on the way to put offense to sleep. An hour or so later, at the opening-night party, Jim Proctor grabbed my arm and pulled me to a phone. On the other end was the whispered voice of Sam Zolotow, that generation's theatrical inside dopester and a reporter for the *Times*, who was actually reading our review directly off Brooks Atkinson's typewriter as the critic wrote it—I could hear the clacking of the typewriter on the phone. In his Noo Yawk voice he excitedly whispered word after word as Atkinson composed it under his nose—"Arthur Miller has written a superb drama. From every point of view, it is rich and memorable . . ."—and as one encomium was laid upon another Sam's voice grew more and more amazed and warm and he seemed to reach out and give me his embrace. The conspiracy that had begun with me and spread to Kazan, the cast, Mielziner, and all the others now extended to Zolotow and Atkinson and the *Times*, until for a moment a community seemed to have formed of people who cared very much that their common sense of life in their time had found expression.

GEORGE P. CASTELLITTO ON *SALESMAN* AS POLITICAL COMMENTARY

If the tragedy of Willy Loman in *Death of a Salesman* is merely the outcome of the conflict between his inner selves and his many-sided persona and if the dramatic rhythm of the play revolves around Willy's inability to distinguish between his inner world and external reality (Hadomi 157), then the play becomes no more than an expressionistic and allegorical representation of the failure of capitalism and of the ravages that the deterministic materialism of modern capitalist society inflicts on individual consciousness. What Willy experiences throughout the play is the enigma of the tension between Marxist socialism and capitalism; he comprehends that capitalism and its tenets (its several accouterments, its technological devices, its progressive westerly movement to a vanished frontier, its commodity-based philosophical foundation) are both ineffective and inutile. However, despite traditional critical stances that portray Willy as the possibly noble "drummer" whom "nobody dast blame" and who "never knew who he was" (138), Willy does not persist as the failed product of the elusive American Dream but as the man whose unconscious yearnings for the safety of socialism transport him to a point, both metaphysically and psychologically, where the sociological tension between that socialism and the capitalism that Willy has been taught to embrace forces him to the crisis that leads to his suicide. In effect, Willy fails because both socialism and capitalism have failed in the modern world, for neither offers the individual a specific place in the social and metaphysical cosmos that fulfills that individual's needs for financial stability, meaningful relationships, and self actualization. If the Marxist tenet is indeed veridical that "truth" is not eternal but rather conceived institutionally, then the institutional "truth" of Willy Loman's life emanates from the tension between the Marxist socialism that he craves and the capitalist notion of success that inflicts its exacting requirements on his psyche. . . .

Willy's disdain for the substantive products and isolationist wanderings indigenous to capitalism and his yearnings for the family cohesiveness that existed a decade earlier become the catalysts that propel him from his expressionistic musings to his realistic discernment that capitalism has failed, at least for the needs of his psyche. Willy's life has been, and continues to be until his suicide, an attempt to produce, and yet his yield has been minimal, slight, frustrating, and elusive. In his assessment of Marx's socialist doctrine, Louis Althusser in *Pour Marx* asserts that production is the transformative foundation of all social activity; therefore, in the confines of the specific dicta that emanate from capitalist philosophy, Willy's striving for production has been a failure and yet simultaneously an ironic sidling toward a socialist stance in which production does not need to provide financial success but rather render for the producer an association with the individuals in the social unit. Eric Mottram explains how Miller highlights the "conflict between a man and his society through a system of language which repeats ordinary catch-phrases and shared jargon, manipulated to cover the facts" (29). *Salesman* employs the habitual language of the commodity-based consciousness of 1949 to accentuate the prevalence of production in a capitalist society and to display how, ironically, the system of capitalist production has failed for Willy, despite the supposed commonness of both the "things" of that society and of the language that attempts to denote those things. In a discussion of "the articulate victims of Arthur Miller," Ruby Cohn indicates that "Willy is not frugal of words, but he has so few of them that he keeps repeating his small stock" (79). Thus, the very language that capitalism produces is itself not only redundant but also insufficient in its ability to reflect the reality of the failure of capitalism, and that "linguistic poverty" that Willy exhibits is emblematic of "both the poverty of his world and the poverty of his dream" (Cohn 75). Willy himself recognizes the inadequacy of both the system of capitalism and the commodity-based language that the system employs, for that capitalistic arrangement concentrates on the production-based assets of the individual and not on the individual worth of the producer. The Althusserian notion of the Marxist conception of production postulates that both individual and collective yield transforms the individual into a viable and indispensable member of socialist society; such a view is a credible stance when examining Willy's dilemma because Willy persists as the almost allegorical embodiment of failed capitalism and frustrated socialism.

Throughout the play, the commodities purchased in the context of capitalism (the machines, the objects, the locations) fail to offer to Willy any enduring and immutable connection with the cosmos and with others. Besides the Studebaker's and the refrigerator's tenuous reliability and besides the Loman house being "boxed in" between "bricks and windows, windows and bricks" (17), the machines purchased as emblems of apparent capitalistic success fail as well. In act 2, Howard's recording machine merely rattles off a series of useless information about the capitals of a sprawling continent that contains locations but lacks substance. Typical of a product of capitalism, the recording machine dissipates the family rather than connects it, for, in Howard's insistence that his wife speak into the machine, in her unwillingness to do so, and in the maid interrupting the process, the disassociation inherent in the capitalistic family joined to each other through acquisition of commodities becomes apparent. Willy himself does not trust the machine, and, in his assertion to Howard that he thinks he will get one as well, Willy expresses his mistrust for the very thing for which he yearns. Indeed, the "things" of capitalistic production dissect the owner and the assets rather than connect; this sense of separation from self and from other is characteristic of not only Willy but also Biff, the psychological and sociological product of Willy's sermonizing. The individual at the "moment of crisis" (Williams 319) in which he comprehends the inefficacy of the system that has submerged him finds himself finally forced to choose, and it is the impossibility of that choice, a decision Willy has delayed for decades, that forces him to his crisis and to his suicide. Raymond Williams discusses, in his assessment of Joe Keller in *All My Sons*, how the vacillation between choices generates disconnection and the "classical Marxist concept of alienation" (317). Williams further asserts:

> *Death of a Salesman* takes the moment of crisis in which Joe Keller could only feebly express himself, and makes of it the action of the whole play. [T]he guilt of Willy Loman is not a single act, subject to public process, needing complicated grouping and plotting to make it emerge; it is, rather, the consciousness of a whole life. (319)

For Willy, that consciousness itself is comprised of a complicated series of contradictory impulses and realistic correspondences in which he simultaneously yearns for and rejects the very items and their accompanying disparities that beckon him both psychologically and socially. This sense of dissimilitude between Willy's longings and his discernment of the fruitlessness of those aspirations affect the diminishing and subsuming of his stature, the loss of his "size" as M. W. Steinberg explains:

> Willy does not gain "size" from the situation. He is seen primarily as the victim of his society; his warped values, the illusions concerning the self he projects, reflect those of his society. His moments of clear self-knowledge are few. (86)

In the very act of his diminishment, Willy becomes the emblem of failed capitalism and possible socialism; he is no longer like his brother Ben, the expander and conqueror, but rather he is a miniature unit in a massive construct whose parameters and regulations elude him. In effect, Willy is contained by forces similar to those that suppress John Proctor in *The Crucible*, but Willy is not actually consciously aware of those forces as is Proctor.

77

Inherent in the suppression of Willy's individuality and the continuance of his dwindling stature is Miller's notion of the contradictoriness of the American myth of the victory of individual consciousness (Kintz 110). If the individual cannot discover connection and personal worth in a commodity-based system, then (Miller is implying) the individual must reject that system and seek another. However, that rejection and that seeking are exactly what Willy is not clearly able to accomplish. Linda Kintz explains that:

Willy's internalizing of the jumbled myths that surround success point to a particular opposition; the relation between style and substance, a relation that initially presupposes substance but at every turn finds style and appearance to be poised over emptiness. (110)

Willy's unconscious leanings dictate to him the manifest emptiness and hollowness of the substantive verities of his existence. Indeed, several critics recognize that Biff's disdain for the pen proceeds naturally as a psychological extension of Willy's contempt for capitalist-based articles that either continuously break down or fail to provide consequential relationships with "other"—the automobile, the refrigerator, the unpredictable recording machine, the stockings that Linda mends and that Willy gives to Miss Francis, the mortgaged home that is now practically empty, the fallow back yard where nothing grows. In both Willy's and the play's unconscious predilection for socialist parameters, Miller is manifesting the failure of the substance of capitalism and displaying the *possibility* of a Socialist consciousness that discerns that submergence in a self-actualizing system where individuals are joined for a type of Althusserian, production-based, transformative, connective existence is preferable to the diminishment of individual stature that occurs in a capitalist system.

In his discussion of the play as "an attack on American institutions and values," Leonard Moss enumerates the several "things" of capitalism that serve as the "sources of corruption" that undermine and eventually destroy Willy: the allure of gadgets that attract and fail, the machismo of American athletic competition, the possession of women as sexual objects, the lack of ethics in business transactions, and the concept of authority and control (Moss quoting from Stallknecht 35–6). *Salesman* is not the first play in which Miller condemns American capitalist practices and the corruption that those customs induce, but Willy is the first character to stand poised on a cliff where the tenets of socialism, however they may be implied within the framework of the play, seem preferable to the principles of the capitalism toward which he strives. Even though Willy comprehends that such a striving is ultimately a gradual progression to his doom, he is compelled to follow the canon of capitalist ideals that he has taught his sons, that has followed him from his youth, that he both despises and covets. The enigma of Willy suspended between the two systems becomes one of the essential and ambivalent elements of the play's capability to allow the reader to apprehend Miller's struggle to reconcile the conflict between a socialism that could prove beneficial and a capitalism that had only proven vituperative.

Works Cited

Althusser, Louis. *Pour Marx*. Trans. Ben Brewster. Verso Books, 1965.

Cohn, Ruby. *Dialogue in American Drama*. Indiana UP, 1971.

Demastes, William W. "Miller's Use and Modification of the Realist Tradition." *Approaches to Teaching Miller's* Death of a Salesman. Ed. Matthew C. Roudané. New York: Modern Language Association, 1995, 74–81.

Hadomi, Leah. "Fantasy and Reality: Dramatic Rhythm in *Death of a Salesman*." *Modern Drama* 31.2 (June 1988): 157–74.

Kintz, Linda. "The Sociosymbolic Work of Family in *Death of a Salesman*." *Approaches to Teaching Miller's* Death of a Salesman. Ed. Matthew C. Roudané. New York: Modern Language Association, 1995, 102–114.

Miller, Arthur. *The Theater Essays of Arthur Miller*. Ed. Robert A. Martin. New York: Viking Press, 1978.

———. *Timebends: A Life*. New York: Harper & Row, 1987.

———. *Death of a Salesman*. New York: Penguin, 1949.

Moss, Leonard. *Arthur Miller*. Boston: Twayne, 1980.

Mottram, Eric. "Arthur Miller: The Development of a Political Dramatist in America." *Arthur Miller: A Collection of Critical Essays*. Ed. Robert W. Corrigan. Englewood Cliffs: Prentice-Hall, 1969, 23–57.

Steinberg, M. W. "Arthur Miller and the Idea of Modern Tragedy."
Arthur Miller: A Collection of Critical Essays. Ed. Robert W.
Corrigan. Englewood Cliffs: Prentice-Hall, 1969, 81–93.

Williams, Raymond. "The Realism of Arthur Miller." *Arthur Miller:
Death of a Salesman, Text and Criticism.* Ed. Gerald Weales. New
York: Viking Press, 1967, 313–25.

STEVEN R. CENTOLA ON UNITY
AND OPPOSITION IN *SALESMAN*

In writing about his search for the appropriate form for
this play, Miller explains why he decided it was necessary to
incorporate paradox into his dramatic strategy. Miller says:

> I sought the relatedness of all things by isolating their
> unrelatedness, a man superbly alone with his sense of not
> having touched and finally knowing in his last extremity
> that the love which had always been in the room unlocated
> was now found. The image of a suicide so mixed in motive
> as to be unfathomable and yet demanding statement . . .
> the image of private man in a world full of strangers. . . .
> I aimed to make a play with the veritable countenance of
> life. To make one the many, as in life, so that "society" is a
> great power and a mystery of custom and inside the man
> and surrounding him, as the fish is in the sea and the sea
> inside the fish, his birthplace and burial ground, promise
> and threat. . . . (*Introduction to Collected works* 30–31)

Miller's comments reveal his conscious decision to unite
oppositional forces in his play and use the play's form, which
mirrors and embodies Willy's internal conflict, as the primary
means of showing the underlying tension that results from the
reciprocal pull of dialectical forces in his principal character's
life. Willy's situation, though, while extraordinary in many
respects, may ultimately be more representative than we
might like to admit. Most people at some time in their lives
feel the powerful force of society operating within them as

they struggle against its pressure to conform and attempt to maintain their individuality. Likewise, at some point we all sense the surge of time endlessly flowing in our minds as memories mingle with conscious thought patterns or take surrealistic shape in dreams. Past and present certainly live within all of us. The contradictory impulses that wage a war inside Willy Loman are the bane of human existence. *Salesman*'s success, therefore, lies in Miller's ability to find a form that not only reveals the inner workings of Willy Loman's disoriented mind, but that also comments on the paradoxical condition that defines human existence: the constant struggle within the individual between self and society, right and wrong, love and hate, consciousness and unconsciousness, success and failure, joy and sorrow, work and play, past and present, life and death. Life is flux and, and as Miller, O'Neill, and other great writers have repeatedly demonstrated, human life is frequently characterized by internal conflict. If the value of a human life may ultimately be determined by the extent to which an individual struggles against contradictory impulses in an effort to give existence purpose and meaning, then it is easy to see why *Death of a Salesman* is so popular and successful and still continues to move audiences all around the world. Willy's battle is ours too, for despite his particular failings and idiosyncrasies, Willy Loman's futile effort to resist reduction and atomization and his constant flight from his alienated condition reflect a universal need for personal triumph over the forces that deny individuality and constantly threaten to diminish our humanity.

This condition of tension that Miller captures in the form of *Death of a Salesman* is evident in virtually every aspect of the play. It is inherent in the complex interrelationship between opposed loyalties and ideals in Willy's mind that motivate every facet of his speech and behavior. It is evident as well in the dramatic interplay between Willy and other characters in the play, not only those present—like Biff, Happy, and Linda Loman, but also significant figures mentioned by Willy who have helped to shape his values or have played some role in the formation of his personality and sense of self-esteem—such as his father, his brother, Ben, and his greatest inspiration: Dave Singleman. The condition of tension can also be seen in the play's unusual style—Miller's remarkable fusion of realism and expressionism—as well as in the unity of text and subtext, image and word, gesture and sound, music and lighting, reality and illusion, and character and action in the play. Miller combines expressionism—in the lighting, music, distorted time sequence, and surrealistic scenes with Ben—with the psychological realism most vividly found in Willy's characterization through such aspects of his behavior as his gestures, intonation, speech rhythms, facial expressions, and body language. Through his careful integration of the realistic and surrealistic aspects of the play, Miller not only allows his audience to see the inner workings and strange logic of Willy's mind, but he does so in such a way that ensures that everything Willy says and does retains a strong sense of probability. In this way, what is essentially impossible to view in a realistic manner—the stream of consciousness inside a person's head—is presented to the audience in viable dramatic terms.

This dialectical tension is also present in other ways. As the action unfolds and Willy plods unyieldingly toward the suicide that he views as his personal triumph, the spellbound audience cannot help but anticipate the eventual outcome while simultaneously wishing that what must come to pass will never occur. The audience feels the force of necessity that governs Willy's actions even while observing the salesman's irrational resistance to the factors that control his destiny. This clash between the actual and the imagined works on us subliminally and affects our response to Willy's dilemma. We come to understand and perhaps even share his desperate conviction that he must at once both pursue and yet hide from the truth. Everything presented in the play contributes in some way to the audience's awareness of the condition of tension that defines *Salesman*'s form and vision. . . .

Miller displays the gravity of Willy's glide into his private world of dreams and illusions through his use of the surrealistic scenes in which Willy reenacts the past. In these memory scenes, Miller suggests that Willy's inner division has much to do with his confusion over his identity and his uncertainty about value formation. Abandoned at an early age by his father, Willy has tried all of his life to compensate for this painful loss. This early experience of betrayal and abandonment is compounded by the equally disturbing disappearance of his older brother. With the two men from his childhood family virtually abandoning him as they venture off in search of their own personal dreams, Willy finds himself alienated from the community of men and nearly completely loses his sense of his own identity as a male. His insecurity about his identity is evident in the memory scene where he confesses to Ben that he feels "kind of temporary" (*Salesman* 159) about himself and seeks his brother's assurance that he is doing a good job of bringing up his sons. "I'm afraid that I'm not teaching them the right kind of—Ben, how should I teach them?" asks Willy (*Salesman* 159). However, even though Willy seems to idolize Ben and treasure his advice and opinions, Willy rarely does what Ben suggests. In fact, until the end of act 2, when Ben appears entirely as a figment of Willy's troubled imagination in a scene that has little to do with any remembered episode from the past, Willy implicitly rejects Ben's lifestyle and approach to business. Ben, therefore, embodies more than just the image of success in Willy's mind; in many ways, he can be viewed as Willy's alter ego. Ben is the other self that Willy might have become had he decided to live by a different code of ethics. For, unlike Ben, who abandoned the family and screwed on his fists to fight for his fortune in Alaska and Africa, Willy stayed in Brooklyn with his family—perhaps even cared for his mother before her death—and embraced a different approach to business than that which is exemplified by his brother. Willy turned to a model from the past and patterned his life on Dave Singleman's example: the legendary eighty-four-year-old salesman who sold merchandise in thirty-one states by picking up his telephone in his hotel room and calling buyers who loved him. Just as Ben is the embodiment of one kind of American dream to Willy, so too is Dave Singleman representative of another kind—and that dichotomy is also part of Willy's confusion: both men symbolize the American dream, yet in Willy's mind they represent value systems that are diametrically opposed to each other. The memory scenes, therefore, are important in bringing out this contrast and in showing what Willy's thoughts about Ben reflect about his own conflicting values.

Miller further uses the memory scenes to display the condition of tension by showing how the weight of Ben's authority in Willy's mind is counterbalanced by the equally powerful influence of other characters. This counterbalancing effect seems designed to show that, while Ben has had a significant impact on Willy's past that continues to remain alive in the present in his imagination, Ben's influence on Willy over the years has actually been no greater than that which has been exerted upon him by such characters as Linda and Dave Singleman, who perhaps had the most profound impact on Willy since he exists in Willy's mind exclusively as an idealized image.

Throughout *Death of a Salesman*, Miller externalizes warring factions within Willy's fractured psyche through the dynamic and oftentimes contentious interaction of the play's characters. Each character essentially expresses a different part of Willy's personality. Linda stirs his guilt and pricks his conscience with her loyalty, devotion, and affection; Charley's common sense and practicality pull Willy toward an honest confrontation with his situation; Ben's pride and arrogance reflect Willy's own egotistical drive for self-assertion and self-fulfillment; Biff gives voice to Willy's own poetic struggle for meaning and purpose in life; Happy, on the other hand, merely verbalizes Willy's lies, dreams, and self-delusion. These forces fiercely compete against each other, struggling for dominance over Willy, but although one might temporarily rise in prominence over the others, no one maintains control indefinitely. All remain active within Willy, leaving him divided, disturbed, and confused.

And, significantly, Willy is not the only character in *Salesman* who experiences this condition. In his stage directions, Miller describes both Biff and Happy as "*lost*" and "*confused*" (*Salesman* 136). They have inherited different parts of Willy's personality and have acquired both his powerful dreams and their society's myths, but they also lack any genuine understanding of how best to attain their own American dream. Happy completely succumbs to the lure of the cultural myth of success, but after wrestling with his conscience and deciding not to conform to his father's expectations and live his lies, Biff momentarily shatters the Loman life-lie in an effort to free himself and save his father's life. Ironically, this very act of love serves as the catalyst for Willy's death. After suffering years of guilty torment and self-punishment, Willy gets concrete proof of his son's love. Rather than risk losing the precious but tenuous connection that now binds him to Biff, Willy decides to end his life and guarantee that he will no longer incur the wrath, condemnation, and scorn of those he truly loves. The Requiem scene, however, implies that his suicide may have had the opposite effect of what it was designed to achieve.

Standing over his father's grave, Biff rejects Willy's life and says: "He had all the wrong dreams. All, all, wrong . . . He never knew who he was" (*Salesman* 221). The play shows that Biff is at least partially right. Willy does deny the value of his aptitude for manual labor, and he lives his life pursuing false dreams and running away from his responsibility for his failures and failings. However, Biff only sees part of the picture. Charley is also right in saying: "A salesman is got to dream, boy. It comes with the territory" (*Salesman* 222). While Charley may literally be referring to the necessity to embrace the dream of success in American society as a cultural inheritance that drives the capitalist establishment, Miller deliberately plants this important speech at the play's end to emphasize the inescapable conditions of human existence that compel us all to dream. The territory Charley alludes to really belongs to all of us. It is the psychic map of humanity that makes us long for an unalienated existence and a life that is not devoid of purpose and meaning. Miller's vivid use of a metaphorical contrast best describes our alienated condition. He says: "We wish so for a pillow to lay our head upon, and it's a stone" (*Conversation* 29). Life is change, conflict, tension, a war of wills and desires, an everlasting struggle to bring order to chaos and impose meaning on a fundamentally absurd world. It is the entropic condition that Willy resists, and because of Willy's fierce determination to fight his impossible battle against the inherent conditions of life and human existence, Miller writes: "There is a nobility . . . in Willy's struggle. Maybe it comes from his refusal to relent, to give up" (*Beijing* 27). Against all odds, Willy demands that life have "meaning and significance and honor" (*Beijing* 49). Willy, says Miller, "is trying to lift up a belief in immense redeeming human possibilities" (*Beijing* 29). This is the attraction and glory of Willy Loman, and this limitless hope in the face of hopelessness is also what ultimately defines the tragic spirit of Miller's vision in *Death of a Salesman*.

Works Cited

Barnes, Howard. "A Great Play Is Born." *New York Theatre Critics' Reviews*. Ed. Rachel W. Coffin 10 (1949): 360.

Bigsby, Christopher. "Arthur Miller: Poet." *Michigan Quarterly Review* 37 (Fall 1998): 713–724.

Brantley, Ben. "Attention Must Be Paid, Again." *New York Times* 11 February 1999: B1, B5.

Centola, Steve. *Arthur Miller in Conversation*. Dallas: Northouse & Northouse, 1993.

Coleman, Robert. "'*Death of a Salesman*' Is Emotional Dynamite." *New York Theatre Critics' Reviews*. Ed. Rachel W. Coffin 10 (1949): 360.

Jackson, Esther Merle. "*Death of a Salesman*: Tragic Myth in the Modern Theatre." *College Language Association Journal* 7 (September 1963): 63–76.

Miller, Arthur. *Death of a Salesman*. *Arthur Miller's Collected Plays*. Vol. 1. New York: Viking, 1957. 129–222.

———. Introduction. *Arthur Miller's Collected Plays*. Vol. 1. New York: Viking, 1957. 3–55.

———. *Salesman in Beijing*. New York: Viking, 1984.

Morehouse, Ward. "Triumph at the Morosco." *New York Theatre Critics' Reviews*. Ed. Rachel W. Coffin 10 (1949): 360.

Shales, Tom. "Spellbinding '*Salesman*' on CBS." *The Washington Post* 14 September 1985: C1, C7.

Shickel, Richard. "Rebirth of an American Dream." *New York Theatre Critics' Reviews*. Eds. Joan Marlowe and Betty Blake 45 (1984): 330.

Watt, Douglas. "Scott in Miller's '*Salesman*.'" *New York Theatre Critics' Reviews*. Eds. Joan Marlowe and Betty Blake 36 (1975): 221.

TERRY W. THOMPSON ON BIFF AS THE HERCULES OF BROOKLYN

Although not an educated, erudite, or worldly man, Willy Loman does, on a few occasions during *Death of a Salesman*, offer modest literary or contemporary allusions. For example, when he conjures up a vivid memory of Biff—the favorite of his two sons—back in the glory days of his youth, Willy visualizes the superb young athlete with a large capital "S" on his letterman's sweater, alluding, of course, to Superman, the popular comic book and movie serial hero. As the star football player on his high school team, Biff certainly was a local super hero of sorts—good-looking, charismatic, athletically gifted, clearly destined for future greatness in professional sports, politics, business, anything and everything he chose to tackle after high school. In praise of Biff's youthful promise, Willy offers an important if brief mythological allusion to one of the most beloved of all Greek heroes, but, like the aging salesman himself, the reference is rather shallow, ignorant, and uninformed, proving that Willy Loman knows as little about classical mythology as he does about business or management or public relations.

At the end of Act One, as he engages in another of his emotionally draining recollections of the family's rose-tinted yesterdays when all things were possible, Willy describes how Biff looked as a muscular teenage heartthrob, boasting that his older boy was "Like a young god, Hercules—something like that."[1] Without even realizing it, Willy has made an ironic yet appropriate mythological allusion, one that he sees as fitting on the surface, but one that is complex, even profound, when examined more closely. As Willy mentions this comparison to Linda, his wife, he intends for the simile to conjure up only the heroic image of Hercules as a strong, fearless, universally admired figure, and certainly the revered Greek demigod embodied all of those positive attributes along with a multitude of others. However, Willy does not, perhaps cannot, comprehend the deeper, darker meanings of his comparison as well as the ironic suitability of his paralleling of Biff with "the greatest of all the Greek heroes."[2]

Born half divine, Hercules was the son of Zeus by a mortal woman, Alcmene of Argolis. Immediately after the birth of Hercules, Zeus neglected the boy and the mother—embarrassed by the consequences of his philandering and also unwilling to accept the daunting responsibilities of full-time fatherhood. In addition, Zeus's duties as king of all the Olympian gods caused much of his time to be taken up with the demands of his high position. As a result, Hercules, "the strongest man on earth," spent almost all of his childhood and formative years without a father figure, without an older, wiser male to give advice, to answer questions, in short, to teach him how to be a man.[3] Raised by a concerned mother who loved but could not control her son, the myths of Hercules are rich with the many problems and difficulties of the boyish giant trying to grow up on his own without a father around to provide male guidance and, when necessary, strong masculine discipline. In effect, Hercules grows up without limits, without corrections on his misbehavior, since no one dares to tell him "No."

Likewise, Biff Loman grows up without a full-time father in his life, especially during his rebellious adolescent years when he was stealing footballs, cheating on exams, driving illegally, and roughing up school girls until, according to Linda, "All the mothers [were] afraid of him!" (Miller 40). During much of Biff's childhood, Willy was off in his Studebaker or Chevrolet, traveling the back roads and byways of New England, leaving his two muscular and headstrong sons to fend for themselves. On one of Willy's much-anticipated arrivals back home, Biff greets him with "Where'd you go this time, Dad? Gee, we were lonesome for you [. . .]. Missed you every minute" (30). Willy's dedication to bread winning for the family is, of course, completely admirable, but his habitual absences—as well as his Zeus-like infidelity while in Boston—have a traumatic effect on his two boys, but most especially on Biff. Willy's homecomings are extremely special events in the childhood of young Biff, but they are infrequent and not enough to keep the boisterous young boy on the straight and narrow path. Willy promises Biff that "Someday I'll have my own business, and I'll never have to leave home any more" (30). That admirable vow, however, never comes to pass, and Biff's self-guided childhood and rebellious adolescence prove to have a negative effect on him as he tries—without success—to become a mature, responsible man. Similarly, Zeus did, on rare occasions, come down from high Olympus to aid or encourage his wayward, troublesome son, and though much appreciated, these few visits were no replacement for a full-time father during Hercules's important formative years.

Throughout his tragic and troubled life, the powerful Greek hero failed at practically everything he attempted since, although incredibly athletic and supernaturally strong, "Intelligence did not figure largely in anything he did and was often conspicuously absent" (Hamilton 160). Handsome, well-built, charismatic, likable, all the attributes that Willy Loman believes guarantee success, these were present in Hercules as well as in the young Biff, but they are merely surface qualities, and unfortunately Willy can never get beyond that surface—in the business world or in the greater world at large. Modern television and movie treatments notwithstanding, when the myths of Hercules are studied in their entirety in Ovid, Virgil, Pindar, Plautus, et al., the tales are often poignant and forlorn, quite moving in their sadness and their pathos. For instance, Hercules married, sired several healthy children, but then he murdered his entire family in a fit of madness. He married a second time, and the wife from that union unintentionally caused him to suffer the agonizing, flesh-eating wounds that would drive him to commit suicide. Realizing what she had done, she hanged herself in despair. During his short life, Hercules also killed a number of people by accident, some of them close friends and companions, causing him tremendous guilt and shame. For the most part, he wandered through the classical world alone, failing at almost every turn to fit in, to find his place. Assigned by the gods as penance for his many sins, the infamous Twelve Labors took Hercules far and wide— and when accomplished gave him great fame—yet he died alone without family or friends to comfort him. His days were punctuated by occasional brief periods of contentment, but overall his life was filled with loneliness and pain, depression and disappointment, so much so that in the end, the "earth's champion," as Ovid describes him, decided to cremate himself on the summit of Mount Oeta in central Greece.[4]

At the end of Act One, when Willy tosses off his clichéd and cursory allusion to the famous Greek hero-athlete, he understands nothing of the darker elements of the Hercules myths, yet they are the very ones that so closely correspond with Biff's unhappy life and his failure to find a place in the world. Willy's own mythological allusion is presumably over his head, demonstrating the shallowness of his erudition and insight and echoing his lack of real acumen about the business world in which, after a lifetime of work, he has proven so inept and unsuccessful. At the age of sixty-three, at a time in his life when he should be able to offer sage and mature counsel to Biff, Willy remains simplistic and superficial, well intentioned and caring, yet still woefully ignorant of almost all things, even his own allusions.

Notes

1. Arthur Miller, *Death of a Salesman: Certain Private Conversations in Two Acts and a Requiem* (New York: Viking, 1949) 68. All further references will be documented parenthetically within the text.

2. Lillian Feder, *Crowell's Handbook of Classical Literature* (New York: Harper Colophon, 1964) 161.

3. Edith Hamilton, *Mythology: Timeless Tales of Gods and Heroes* (New York: Mentor, 1969) 160.

4. Ovid, *The Metamorphoses*, trans. Mary M. Innes (New York: Penguin, 1955) 209.

DANA KINNISON ON FEMALE STEREOTYPES IN THE PLAY

Male characters dominate Arthur Miller's *Death of a Salesman*. Their presence and concerns take center stage, literally and figuratively. In both those scenes that occur in the present time of 1949 and those relived through memory of the past,

Willy Loman and his sons reveal their dreams and desires, their successes, and especially their failures. Willy is admired by his wife and two young boys, who have a blind faith in his authority and who loyally follow his lead. In the early years, he is competitive and confident, even a braggart, who anticipates fighting his way to the top of the business world just as he encourages his son Biff to aggressively overwhelm opponents on the gridiron. Willy assumes a sense of entitlement, which he in turn engenders in his sons. The aging Willy is bewildered by his inability to realize his dreams and clings even more desperately to his authoritarian, patriarchal ways.

Overshadowed by Willy's grandiose nature is Linda, long-suffering wife and mother. Linda epitomizes the notion of female passivity, caretaking, and self-sacrifice. She stands by her man, seldom questioning and never opposing him. Linda occasionally notices the discrepancies between Willy's exaggerated claims and the reality of their circumstances, but she seems to have neither the desire nor the force of will to counter his distorted perceptions. She is not without insight at times, but her worthwhile observations go unheeded. Although her husband and sons love and even admire her, they do so while simultaneously disregarding her as a full person. Unlike Willy's character, the reader does not know Linda's dreams and desires or, worse, suspects she has none that extend beyond what is in this case a limiting role as wife and mother. Miller affords her less complexity than Willy or Biff, and her lesser status is tied to her gender. If Willy is the magnificently plumed male peacock, loudly proclaiming his sense of self, Linda follows suit and is a plain, quiet pea hen, in attendance but little noticed.

Adolescent readers don't always fully appreciate Miller's flawed and tragic hero. However, it is at least apparent to them that his suffering is worthy of academic discussion, and that he is an ironically forceful figure, a powerful dreamer though not an effective executor of those dreams. Linda, in contrast, lacks any power. Most students are scornful of her gullibility and non-assertion. Willy may be a pathetic as well as a sympathetic character, but Linda is a pitiful "doormat," trod upon by husband and sons alike. Understandably, female students not only resist identification with Linda but sometimes resist full interaction in the classroom if Linda's secondary status is not adequately addressed.

The few other representations of women only serve to compound the problematic messages that the play sends about gender. The character known as The Woman accepts and, indeed, expects Willy's gifts of new hosiery after she spends time with him in a hotel room. The image of The Woman and her new silk stockings is juxtaposed with the image of Linda mending her worn stockings. The old, mended stockings symbolize not only Linda's life of toil and self-sacrifice but also the ignorance and betrayal that mark her existence. These two female figures demonstrate the limited and stereotyped options advanced in many artistic and cultural depictions of women, the polarized madonna/whore syndrome. The other son, Happy, helps to illuminate this point. He wants to marry a good woman like his mother but dates a different sort of woman, as he sees it. Furthermore, he speaks of women in disparaging ways, lies to them, and treats them like sport, winning them away from other men as trophies. If such simplistic and invalidating representations of women go unchallenged, all students suffer, but especially formative young women who need female complexity and potential reflected in literature to aid personal development and esteem.

Is, then, *Death of a Salesman* to be avoided at all costs in the gender-conscious classroom? The answer is no, although to avoid explicitly engaging the abuses and omissions of women in the play is to reinforce sexual inequality. The (non)role that women enact may instead serve as a catalyst for discussions that speak directly to students' lives and to the central concerns of the play itself. First, gender issues may be used as a way of drawing students to the text rather than alienating them. Miller's characters illustrate the elemental power imbalance between the sexes which is at the heart of all varieties of women's marginalization and oppression, large and small, historical and contemporary. If students naively see Linda's domestic subjugation as passé, have them consider Happy's dating practices (his objectification and sexual exploitation of women), which may be closer to young readers' experiences. Also, students might list examples of the madonna/whore syndrome from contemporary popular sources, beginning with the pop star Madonna. Her name calls forth the venerated mother of God, saintly and, well, like a virgin. However, her erotic image and shameless antics are more worthy of a Jezebel. Madonna purposefully exploits the sharply divided choices that have marked female experience.

Next, the play's theme may be addressed. The play is a critique of values embodied in the American Dream: consumerism, competition, and frontierism—including freedom, the acquisition of wealth, and dominance. To be sure, acknowledge that women's subordination in the play parallels their minor role in the dream itself, which is the emanation of a white male ethos. But also critique this very omission as the basis of extended discussion. How might the American Dream have been different if it were influenced by a female ethos? To what extent is the dream's failure (as it is presented in the play) the result of the absence of these traditionally female values? Is the American Dream different today and, if so, how has it been influenced by the changing roles of women? The reading becomes more accessible and more worthwhile for students of both sexes if the absence of forceful female characters is addressed and thus redeemed.

Works Cited
Miller, Arthur. *Death of a Salesman*. New York: Viking, 1949.

For Further Reading
Roudané, Matthew C., ed. *Approaches to Teaching Miller's* Death of a Salesman. New York: Modern Language Association, 1995.

ENOCH BRATER ON THE FIRST PERFORMANCES OF *SALESMAN*

In 1949 Miller took the train from Penn Station in New York to Philadelphia for the tryout of a strange new play he had originally thought of calling *The Inside of His Head*. From early on, the work seemed to demand a stage solution as difficult as it was elusive: how to render the past, the present and the protagonist's increasingly desperate imagination as one continuous whole, without resorting to "flashbacks" (a term the playwright disliked) or the clumsy apparatus of frequent and intrusive scene breaks. The drama would be realistic, of course, but it presupposed a realism with a difference. The naturalistic sets Miller imagined for *All My Sons* and *The Man Who Had All the Luck* would not do the trick here. To make this play work, stage space would have to be explored differently by Miller, the director Elia Kazan and the brilliant and innovative designer Jo Mielziner. This much-celebrated collaboration resulted in the invention of a highly atmospheric platform set that gave *Salesman* the look and flexibility its narrative energy required. On a multi-level constructivist set, time past and time present could be in dialogue with each other as a rhythmic pattern of negotiation and renewal emerged. All that was needed to signal transition was stage lighting, accompanied by the haunting sound of a flute playing somewhere in the distance. Given such a highly unusual design concept, Miller's "dream rising out of reality" might well stand the chance of finding a place for itself on the modern stage.

No one involved in the original production of *Death of a Salesman*, least of all the playwright, was sure that the gamble would work. The producer Kermit Bloomgarden, one of the play's principal backers, recommended a different title for the play. Convinced that no one would buy a ticket to a show with "death" advertised on the marquee, he suggested *Free and Clear*, highlighting Linda's monologue in the Requiem, which brings closure to the play. "The work I wrote is called *Death of a Salesman*," the playwright is reported to have said. When the curtain came down on the first performance at the Locust Theatre in Philadelphia, followed by too many moments of awkward silence, the tension, as Miller relates in his autobiography, was palpable and real. A lot was at stake, not only for Miller, but "for the future of the American theater." There was, finally, thunderous applause, followed by the oddest thing of all: "men and women wept openly" and, after the applause died down, "members of the audience refused to leave and started talking to complete strangers about how deeply they had been affected by the play." Miller, who thought he had written a tough, hard-hitting exposé of the dangerous and deceptive myth of "making it in America," was entirely unprepared for the emotional punch *Salesman* delivered in performance. His play had all at once found a life of its own.

When Willy Loman, suitcase in hand, slowly walks onto the set of *Death of a Salesman* in one of the most famous stage entrances in theater history, he begins the long requiem that finally declares itself as such in the closing moments of the play. The work, Miller said, "is written from the sidewalk instead of from a skyscraper." Unlike Willy's sons, the audience hardly needs to wait for Linda's pronouncement to understand that "the man is exhausted. A small man can be just as tired as a great man." Miller's proletarian spirit permeates the entire play: Willy Loman, the salesman working on commissions that never come, is down on his luck (not that he ever really had any); Happy, who talks big, is the perpetual assistant to an assistant; Biff, who (unlike his father) knows he's "a dime a dozen," is the ageing, fair-haired boy long gone to seed; while Linda, the homebody ignored by time, is unable to stem the tide of tragedy that soon engulfs them all, try as she might. The whole question of "Tragedy and the Common Man" that initially greeted the play, and about which the playwright has perhaps said too much, now seems rather quaint and beside the point in terms of the work's immediacy, accessibility and inter-generational appeal. Linda was right about one thing: "Attention, attention must finally be paid to such a man." . . .

Although we generally think of Miller as a playwright with a narrative rather than a visual imagination, *Death of a Salesman* relies on a strong sense of stage imagery: the set is Miller's play. Dwarfed beneath looming apartment blocks that rob the sunlight from Willy's garden, the Loman house belongs to some other moment in time and a very different sense of place. This is still Brooklyn, but a reimagined Brooklyn in which windows, like dozens of threatening eyes, stare down on a diminished world and make it seem even more local and inconsequential. "There's more people now!" Willy cries out in an anger that is really despair. Most productions of *Salesman* rely on projected scenery to foreground Willy's increasing claustrophobia, yet from a scenic point of view his psychological state is rendered as something palpable, material and frighteningly real. Music, too, tells the story. Each of Willy's journeys into the past, including one double journey, is signaled by the sound of a single, plaintive flute. His father, significantly, made his own flutes by hand, then sold them himself; Willy's sample case, by contrast, contains factory-made "dry goods." Other sounds will be similarly evocative: the recorded voice of a child on tape drowns out Willy's plea for help, and Biff is cautioned against whistling in elevators (he does so anyway; the Lomans are great whistlers). Finally, when Willy's life comes crashing down all around him, we hear the cacophonous sounds of metal twisting, brakes screeching and glass shattering, followed by an ominous stage silence.

In *Salesman*, of course, as elsewhere in Miller, the play's atmospheric dimension is there to enhance the work's narrative authority and appeal. This is first and foremost the theater's most compelling tale of the dark underside of the American Dream, half-fantasy, half phantasmagoria, essentially configured as a triumphalist and everywhere disturbing guy-culture. Willy, as we hear in the play's Requiem, was a man who "never knew who he was"; but he was also, as Miller later said, a man who "chased everything that rusts." He had all "the wrong dreams." Caught up, like most of his country, in the vain and unobtainable lure of success, which he equates with material wealth, popularity and the making of a good impression ("be well liked and you shall never want"), he realizes all too late that what he has been searching for all his life he has had all along: Biff's unqualified love. What makes the play a tragedy—and it is certainly that—is that the father's unfulfilled ambitions, rather than any insurance payouts, are the only inheritance he can offer his sons. His legacy is their peril. "I'm not bringing home any more prizes." What Biff is saying is that you will have to love me anyway. But by then it is too late. Willy drives off and kills himself.

The effect of *Salesman* on Miller's audience can be so daunting, the emotion it excites so raw, that the drama quickly becomes, despite its author's stated intentions, something quite different from a thesis play. And this may have little to do with the protagonist's socioeconomic situation as a "low-man." The playwright took the name from Fritz Lang's *The Testament of Dr. Mabuse*, the 1933 film in which a detective hopes to redeem himself by exposing a gang of forgers. Duped by them instead, he shouts into a telephone to his former boss, "Lohmann? Help me, for God's sake! Lohmann!" Later in the same film, we meet the crazed detective in an asylum as he shouts into an invisible phone, "Lohmann? Lohmann? Lohmann?" "What the name really meant to me," Miller said, "was a terrified man calling into the void for help that will never come."

Deborah R. Geis on *Salesman* Retold

More than fifty years after its first Broadway production, Arthur Miller's *Death of a Salesman* has become a cultural icon....

What interests me most ... is ... the impact of *Salesman* upon American literary and dramatic consciousness: its more direct appropriation as intertext for a surprising number of new theatrical works. In other words, rather than simply evoking Miller's play by some general thematic means, these works export actual characters (or references to actual characters) from *Salesman*, or they quote, parody or otherwise appropriate Miller's text in explicit references to it as either "real" or as a literary work with which the characters are familiar. This type of intertextuality creates a more dialogical approach to Miller's "masterpiece," one that allows for interrogation and deconstruction of its assumptions about culture and character. While in some sense the appropriation of *Salesman* is still a type of homage, these works enact critical rereadings of Miller's play that enable us to review both *Salesman* and these new texts from a postmodern perspective.

* * *

Rosalyn Drexler's 1984 play *Room 17C* begins, in a sense, before *Salesman* ends, as Willy has not yet committed suicide; rather, it exists in a kind of parallel universe that allows Drexler to rewrite Miller's work to her own liking, and even to recombine it with an entirely different literary text. Rosette Lamont describes Drexler's plays as creating a "semiotics of instability" in which she "destabilizes the accepted forms of discourse, of the dramatic genre as a whole" (ix). In *Room 17C* Linda Loman has now taken over Willy's job as a traveling salesperson and has proven to be far more successful at it than he ever was. Drexler gives her Linda the last name of "Normal" rather than "Loman," the near-anagram underscoring the complicated trajectories of characters (both here and in Miller's play) who aspire to "normal" American ideas of success. In her opening stage directions, Drexler shows that although Linda has crossed from the realm of the domestic to the traditionally masculine realm of the wage-earner we should not infer that she has therefore become liberated from the positions that Miller assigned her:

> Linda has taken over her husband's destiny to be a successful salesman. Her life is still not her own. Her husband keeps calling to check up on her. She has to harden herself. In some way she still is playing his "masochistic" game. Whatever she does pains him. He threatens her with his suicide, but it is she who will die (in the line of duty, burned to a crisp with her sport's "knock-'em-dead" line). (2)

Willy, then, exists as an offstage character, a voice on the phone; the first we hear of him is in a missed connection, as Linda at the beginning of the play tries to reach him but gets no answer. Asserting her financial independence, she tells the operator that it is not a collect call, but one that should be charged to her room. Slightly later, she characterizes Willy as "a traveling salesman and a parasite," saying (with a cynicism that stands in sharp contrast to Miller's Linda), "Well, he's fired now. Got a gold-plated watch to commemorate his masochism," adding that now she's the one "who attends to business" (5).

Paralleling Willy's hotel room liaison in *Salesman*, Linda has a romantic encounter . . . with Sammy Gregor, a "man-sized cockroach," obviously drawn from Kafka's Gregor Samsa in *The Metamorphosis*.[3] Drexler takes pain to emphasize that the cockroach should not be played in "cute" Disneyland fashion with a bug costume; rather, he should exhibit a "bug persona" (nervousness, creeping, crawling) but that for the actor, "a well-worn brown suit will suffice" (2). Linda is attracted to Sammy because of his romantic qualities, his sensuality, his free spirit, his ability to banter with her. Her comments to him continually emphasize his otherness: she calls him "loathsome" (3), says she's "not Walt Disney" (9), and tells him, "I will not let you turn this trip into a Japanese horror film" (10).

Yet Linda also makes it clear that she sees a link between Sammy and Willy: not only—as I mentioned earlier—does she characterize Willy as a "parasite," but she even describes a family photograph in which Willy, also in a brown suit, resembled a cockroach: "At any rate, he was more than willing to be there [at her feet], his body flattened, his head at a tilt as if waiting for some final blow" (11). She points this out after Sammy—in a move that echoes Gregor's fetishizing of the photograph in Kafka's story—tells Linda that he saw her framed photo wrapped in her lingerie, and Linda responds that "family photographs reveal too much" (11). What becomes clear in such interactions is that while Sammy and Willy bear more than a superficial resemblance to one another, Sammy is of a different "species" because of his ability to "read" Linda in ways that Willy (at least as we saw him in *Salesman*) was never able to do. At the same time, Linda's initial physical repulsion toward Sammy (which never wholly subsides) is modified by some sense that there is a possibility for a mutual orality (they eat rare hamburgers from room service together; they engage in verbal sparring) that she and Willy have failed to share. Indeed, when she does get Willy on the phone, she talks to him in a series of clichés that she seems to have absorbed from him and from the discourse of striving for the American dream of successful salesmanship: "Where's your backbone, dammit? Sit up straight, Willy, or no one'll know you're at the table" (8).

In Linda's phone conversations with Willy, Drexler plays directly with the audience's awareness of the plot of *Salesman* in order to create an ironic dialogue between her text and that of Miller's play. When Linda hears that Willy is depressed, she says, "No, no, no! Don't kill yourself, darling! It'd be anti-climactic" (8). And later, when he calls back to tell her that he can't find the instant coffee (confirming that he has not switched roles with her very successfully), she tells him, "Oh, I forgot to remind you to check the water heater. Pan has to be emptied. No, the hose does not lead directly to the gas line. Boy, do you sound depressed" (12). Although Linda constantly reaffirms to Willy how much she misses and loves him, it is clear that she is reciting the lines of a script that she has followed many times before, one that is just as familiar to her as one of her sales pitches. At the same time, since the audience knows the script of *Salesman*, we are caught between horror at the inevitability of Willy's demise and amusement at the extent to which Linda's cynicism rebels so profoundly against the role that Miller wrote for her: does Miller's Linda carry any subtextual resentment of Willy, or does Drexler create an entirely subversive reading of her character?

The key moment of disappointment in his father for Biff comes, in *Salesman*, when he surprises Willy in Boston and finds him with a woman in his hotel room. Drexler translates Linda's version of this story rather differently; as Linda explains to Sammy, "They haven't gotten along since Joey [Drexler's parallel to Biff] walked in on Willy when he was with some woman, somewhere." She continues, "Talk about men putting women on a pedestal! Joey had his dad living on Mount Everest. Poor kid, thought he had to take sides, defend me; I couldn't have cared less" (14). Here Drexler radically reverses our assumption that news of her husband's philandering would be devastating to Linda; she refuses to play victim, yet we also get the sense that her cynicism is born of years of disappointment and ultimately has caused her to withdraw emotionally. In what appears at first to be a repetition of Biff's trauma, Joey walks in and finds Linda with Sammy—and indeed, his shocked reaction at first mirrors that of Biff with Willy—but in this case, it is Linda who rewrites the scenario. Joey makes a speech calling her "the lowest of the low," extending his discourse to apply to womankind: "Woman is a perilous craft, and crafty though she is, cannot avoid the rocks in her path, so ready is she to abandon herself to the elements . . . to wreck what has formerly had direction and buoyancy" (18). Crucially, though, Linda responds, "I hadn't realized that I had raised a woman hater, Joey; and an excessively literary one to boot" (18). By calling attention to the textual nature of Joey's language—as she did by calling Willy's suicide attempt "anti-climactic"—Linda forces a Brechtian distancing between a character's words and deeds. This is a relentless act of demystification that can be read psychologically as her own deepening cynicism and as her enactment of an ongoing critique or revision of the text in which her character is "supposed" to find herself. Joey's education has included "learning" the texts of misogyny couched in literary form, yet it is Linda's direct critique of Joey's text that allows her to assert a different kind of maternal power.

The ending "Requiem" of *Salesman* contrasts the voices of Charley, who responds to Biff's remark that Willy had the wrong kind of dreams with his "Nobody dast blame this man" speech; Happy, who vows to fulfill Willy's dream; and Linda, who says that she can't cry and that she has made the last payment on the house—"We're free" (138–39). Drexler's Linda seems to have found, briefly, a kind of freedom with Sammy at the end of *Room 17C*, but it is short-lived. At the end of the play, Joey and Sammy manage to escape when the hotel catches on fire, but Linda expires from smoke inhalation when she stays to answer another phone call from Willy. Sammy, who turns and addresses the audience, gets the last words as his monologue evokes the cockroach's mythical ability to survive the unthinkable:

"Even mushroom clouds cannot divert my way of life" (19). He attributes this ability to his lack of imagination: "Linda had imagination. Imagination can accomplish the end of the world" (19). He then sings the "popular roach anthem," which turns out to be set to the tune of "America the Beautiful" (19–20). Drexler thus provides a complex response to *Salesman*'s nostalgic yet tragic commentary on the pressure for bourgeois success in America in the years after World War II as conveyed through Willy's longings and failure. The survivor in Drexler's play is Sammy, the character who has deliberately chosen an "alternative" path; Linda's "imagination" is seen as both what allowed her to dream and ultimately what brought about her destruction.

Notes

3. Drexler also takes on Kafka in her play *Occupational Hazard* (1988; rev. 1992), an adaptation of his story "A Hunger Artist"; the play is included in Rosette Lamont, ed., *Women on the Verge* (New York: Applause, 1993), 1–44.

AUSTIN E. QUIGLEY ON HOW TO MEASURE WILLY LOMAN

Causality . . . is one of the most problematic features of *Death of a Salesman*. The key problem is not the shortage of causal factors but their sheer number and variety, so much so that the play, with its episodic structure, has at times been criticized for failing to make them cohere. At various points in the play, Willy's radical discontentment is explicitly linked to a variety of causes: the rootlessness and alienation of an urban rather than rural way of life (stage set, ii; Ben, 85; Biff and Happy, 22–23, 61; Willy, 122); the growing population with consequently increased competition and reduced space (Willy, 17–18); the changing values of American society (Willy, 81); the underlying economic system (Happy, 24–25); the early loss of a guiding father figure (Willy, 51); Willy's failure as a husband (Willy, 107); his failure as a father (Willy, 93); his failure as a salesman (Willy, 37); his old age (Linda, 57); his lack of self-knowledge

(Biff, 138); his misguided ambitions (Charley, 89); his excessive self-pity (Biff, 56); his unimpressive appearance (Willy, 37); and so on.[5] This diffusion of the causes of Willy's disenchantment with his life can invite us to dismiss the play as one depicting a disgruntled failure, full of hot air and foolish dreams, whose frequent complaints and evident limitations fail to converge into any coherent pattern. The episodic nature of the play, in these terms, serves more to conceal than clarify the implicit structure of the action.

The counterargument, however, is that Willy is, as Biff defiantly asserts, "a dime a dozen" (132) in every respect except the one that Biff cannot quite comprehend: his desire and determination not to be. The diversity of negative evidence and hostile circumstances then serves not so much to muddy the thematic waters as to clarify the scale of Willy's determination to hold onto an aspiration in the face of counter-evidence of every imaginable kind. . . .

The weight and variety of the negative evidence that Willy is unable to evade or ignore, in effect, lend cumulative stature to his unyielding determination to counter that evidence by transcending his constraining circumstances. The strength of this determination is reinforced rather than diminished by Willy's explicit recognition of the desperate strategies to which he resorts to keep the hope alive. Faced with the lowest point in his life and career, Willy acknowledges the strategies of deception and self-deception required to keep his mammoth aspirations alive for himself and his family, in spite of his limitations and theirs:

> *Willy*: I was fired today, . . . I was fired, and I'm looking for a little good news to tell your mother, because the woman has waited and the woman has suffered. The gist of it is that I haven't got a story left in my head, Biff. So don't give me a lecture about facts and aspects. I am not interested. Now what've you got to say to me? (107)

The direct appeal to Biff to provide him with an enabling story rather than with disabling facts is continuous with a disposition to live on the promise of future achievements—achievements that might ratify the family's strengths and minimize their moments of disillusionment. But the promising stories of future achievement are not themselves enough, either to satisfy Willy or to create so powerful a play.

If the encouraging stories Willy collects and invokes to ratify his preferred narrative line involved mere escapism and self-deception, this would be a less significant play. But there is a reality principle at issue here that is fundamental to the play and to Miller's work as a whole. Though it would be difficult to defend Willy against accusations of self-deception, the self-deception is as much strategic as self-indulgent. The solution Biff offers to their problems, self-knowledge based on external evaluation, is thus illuminatingly inadequate:

> *Biff*: What am I doing in an office, making a contemptuous, begging fool of myself, when all I want is out there, waiting for me the minute I say I know who I am. . . . I am not a leader of men, Willy, and neither are you. You were never anything but a hard-working drummer who landed in the ash can like all the rest of them! I'm one dollar an hour, Willy. I tried seven states and couldn't raise it. A buck an hour! Do you gather my meaning? I'm not bringing home any prizes any more, and you're going to stop waiting for me to bring them home! (132)

Biff's claim that in self-knowledge lies satisfaction is countered, of course, by the vehemence of Willy's "I am not a dime a dozen! I am Willy Loman, and you are Biff Loman!" (132), by the life he has lived to keep Biff's debilitating evaluation at bay, and by the death he deploys as a culminating effort to restart the cycle of success for himself and for Biff. And the trouble with Biff's version of self-knowledge is that it is based upon external evaluations that do not include internal values and personal aspirations, which have their own reality claims.

In a world in which everyone grows and changes, the challenge the play presents is one of requiring us to decide when aspirations are unrealistic and/or unworthy. Aspiration, after all, must often lead achievement into being, otherwise new achievements and new achievers would emerge only by chance. Lurking in the background of Biff's remark that Willy had the wrong dreams (138) and of Charley's remark that "a salesman has got to dream, boy" (138) is that characteristic notion of an American dream in which personal and social transformation is a widely shared expectation, an expectation ratified in a great many rags-to-riches stories of the kind exemplified by the career of Willy's brother, Ben. But if aspiration is an enabling aspect of achievement, who is to say when aspiration, necessarily at odds with current reality, is excessive? And the play's episodic structure and competing narrative lines suspend the question in the action along with others it invites the audience to consider.

It is in the play's epilogue that the overall function of the play's episodic structure becomes most clearly apparent, and it is very much one of challenging the audience to locate the appropriate means of measuring Willy's worth. It is evident enough in the play's action that Willy has many failings, is often self-deceived and self-deceiving, and is much misguided about what might constitute worthwhile success. But those limitations provide neither the measure of the man nor the measure of the play. What the epilogue provides to supplement the three stories that have obsessed Willy, one ratified by his firing, another by the event in Boston, and the other by the event at Ebbets Field, are the stories each of the other characters derives from the action and the values each locates in them. For Linda, Willy was a success after all, as he had paid off the mortgage; for Charley, the career of salesman was a destructive choice, and his raising of Bernard to be a bookworm and a within-the-system success exemplifies a set of values different from Willy's; for Happy, the way forward is beating the system by playing with rather than by the rules and doing so better than anyone else; and, as we have seen, for Biff it is a matter of reducing expectations to one aspect of self-knowledge. But the final speech is Linda's, as she both asserts and questions a mode of measuring Willy's value that has sustained her commitment to him, despite all his evident failings:

Linda: Forgive me, dear. I can't cry. I don't know what it is, but I can't cry. I don't understand it. Why did you ever do that? . . . Why did you do it? I search and search and I search, and I can't understand it, Willy. I made the last payment on the house today. Today, dear. And there'll be nobody home. (*A sob rises in her throat.*) We're free and clear. (*Sobbing more fully, released.*) We're free. (*Biff comes slowly toward her.*) We're free. . . . We're free . . . (139)

And, at this point, "*the apartment buildings rise into sharp focus*" (139), reminding us at the end of the play, as they did at the beginning, of the sense of confinement and containment that the realistic aspects of the set provide to Linda's notions of freedom and success and to Willy's larger hopes and aspirations.

The action of the epilogue, however, takes place on the apron at the front of the stage, and the scene is not one circumscribed by the realism of the set: In "clothes of mourning" and accompanied by the beat of "a dead march," the characters "move toward the audience, through the wall-line of the kitchen" and out to "the limit of the apron" (136). And there, closest to the audience, and removed from the realistic set, the characters debate questions of sufficiency and excess:

Linda: I can't understand it. At this time especially. First time in thirty-five years we were just about free and clear. He only needed a little salary. He was even finished with the dentist.

Charley: No man only needs a little salary. (137)

Linda's domestic dreams seem impoverished when compared to Willy's implausible but more grandiose designs. Charley's remark, however, serves not only to raise the question of how much salary should suffice but also how much achievement, recognition, admiration, love, enduring impact and so on should suffice.

Willy's strength and weakness is his inability to locate a satisfactory measure of sufficient achievement, and he died, as he lived, fatally attracted to the notion that happiness consists of endless expectation of better things on the horizon. As Happy puts it: "Dad is never so happy as when he's looking forward to something!" (105). Willy's sense of containment and confinement is all-pervasive, and the "boxed in" neighborhood provides only an example and not a basic cause of his frustration. His preferred narrative line reaches beyond these constraints, and the play's structure and setting follow suit. When the play extends its episodic structure into a stage set whose partial transparency is designed to move the action beyond representational chronology to presentational rearrangement, it opens access to a world beyond the walls, a realm in which the possibilities of action, measurement and value extend beyond anything that the characters and their sociohistorical situation can encompass.

The play begins, as the stage direction puts it, with a melody, played upon a flute, that tells of "grass and trees and the horizon" (11). Much has been made of the grass and trees, but it is to the horizon that the episodic action of the play ultimately directs our attention. When Willy dies, there is no consensus on the stage about how we should measure his strengths and limitations or the ultimate value of the obsessive aspirations for which he is prepared to sacrifice his life. The conversation in the epilogue emerges from the realistic set of the play out onto the apron of the stage and ultimately out into the auditorium, where it will then be extended further.

Notes
5. Arthur Miller, *Death of a Salesman* (New York: Viking Press, 1971. All page references are to this edition.

Gary Harrington on Enriching the Historical Context of *Salesman*

In Arthur Miller's *Death of a Salesman*, Willy Loman's life teems with ghosts. Prominent among these is the ghost of his older brother, Ben, with whom Willy converses at key points in the play, and most important, in the garden late on the evening of Willy's suicide. Other ghosts, literal and metaphorical, also populate Willy's environment: Biff's younger self, Frank Wagner, the young Bernard, Willy's former mistress, and many others form a spectral circle within which Willy revolves and that ultimately closes around him. According to the stage directions, just before Willy's suicide, "*sounds, faces, voices, seem to be swarming in upon him*" (Miller 136).

Even figuratively, Willy is haunted, and particularly by Biff's failure to achieve success as a sports figure. Willy tells Bernard that Biff's "life ended after that Ebbets Field game" (92) and that, when Biff flunked math shortly thereafter, he "laid down and died like a hammer hit him" (93). As Willy also remarks to Bernard, Biff's failures as a student and as a potential sports star have been "trailing me like a ghost for the last fifteen years" (93). Related to Biff's dereliction and to its tormenting of Willy is Willy's prediction to Charlie just before the Ebbets Field game that "they'll be calling [Biff] another Red Grange" (89). Harold Edward "Red" Grange (1903–91) was an All-American halfback at the University of Illinois from 1923–25, and then went on to a very successful, highly lucrative, and heavily publicized career as a professional football player with the Chicago Bears. As Benjamin Rader notes, while not all Americans "were able to see Grange perform in the flesh, millions saw him in the newsreels of thousands of theaters" (141). And as Miller was no doubt aware, Grange's elusiveness as a running back earned him the sobriquet of "The Galloping Ghost," a term that might aptly, if ironically, apply both to Biff's running from responsibility and to the way in which his resultant failures pursue Willy wherever he goes.

One of these failures involves Willy's pawning his diamond watch fob to pay for Biff's radio correspondence course (53), a sacrifice that naturally came to nothing. Perhaps it is no coincidence that, at the time Miller was writing *Death of a Salesman*, Red Grange was enjoying a successful second career as a radio sports commentator. Even the name "Harold" which Hap claims to be his own at Frank's Chop House may derive from Grange, whose own first name was Harold. Interestingly,

Hap makes this claim in the same conversation in which he also maintains that Biff is a professional football player.

Miller might well have found Grange a particularly compelling sports figure to integrate into *Death of a Salesman* because Grange was one of the first to capitalize on his college fame by abandoning his university studies in favor of a high salary as a professional football player. As Brenda Murphy and Susan C. W. Abbotson note, the "transformation of amateur athletics into a business for profit was an issue when Biff Loman [would have been] playing football in the early 1930s [. . .]" (166). Indeed, Grange's jump from the college ranks to the pros occasioned much controversy at the time. Nonetheless, Grange remained unabashed about opting for the pros, stating "I'm out to get the money, and I don't care who knows it [. . .] my advice to everybody is to get to the gate while the getting's good" (qtd. in Rader 142), sentiments that Willy would certainly endorse.

After Willy wrongly predicts that Biff will be "another Red Grange. Twenty-five thousand a year," Charlie asks, "Who is Red Grange?" (89). Most of those in a 1949 audience would, of course, have been able to answer that question. Although presumably few today would be able to do so, raising Grange's galloping ghost for a contemporary audience enriches the texture of one of the most enduringly popular twentieth-century plays.

Works Cited

Miller, Arthur. *Death of a Salesman.* New York: Penguin, 1976.

Murphy, Brenda and Susan C. W. Abbotson. *Understanding "Death of a Salesman."* Westport, CT: Greenwood, 1999.

Rader, Benjamin G. *American Sports.* Upper Saddle River, NJ: Prentice, 1983.

PETER L. HAYS ON THE PLAY'S LANGUAGE

[Critics] Mary McCarthy, Stanley Kauffmann (writing for *The New Republic*), and David Mamet noticed the Yiddish inflections in the dialogue. Kauffmann wrote:

The diction is first-generation Brooklyn Jewish. ('Attention, attention must finally be paid to such a person.') But often the dialogue slips into a fanciness that is slightly ludicrous. To hear Biff say, 'I've been remiss,' or to hear Linda say, 'He was crestfallen, Willy,' is like watching a car run off the road momentarily onto the shoulder. (I've never heard anyone use the word 'crestfallen' in my life.) (Kauffmann, 1976: 142)

But the play's language has its defenders, including Miller himself. In *Salesman in Beijing*, Miller said, 'The Lomans are usually trying *not* to speak "commonly." In fact, their rhetorical flourishes dot the play and are echoes of Willy's vision of himself and Biff transcending into something more classy in life, something like glory' (Miller, 1987: 40; original emphasis). 'His . . . practice,' commented British drama critic and scholar Dennis Welland, 'has usually been to lift the dialogue fractionally above the incoherencies of everyday intercourse while keeping it firmly grounded in the rhythm of ordinary speech and the idiom of the vernacular' (Welland, 1979: 16). According to Brian Parker, 'The language, too, except in a few places, is an accurate record of the groping half inarticulate, cliché-ridden inadequacy of ordinary American speech' (Parker, 1988: 26). Thus the constant repetition of clichés realistically characterizes the Lomans as people of limited education and banal lives. Willy repeats 'well liked' as a mantra that he cannot see beyond, just as Ben in Willy's mind repeats 'And by God I was rich.' And so their flights of rhetoric are indications of great imagination and ambition. Miller is not as lyrical a writer as Tennessee Williams, and critics may have been comparing the two, but the banal prose of his characters does serve well the purpose of characterization.

The phrase 'such a person' and the object first in 'Attention, attention must finally be paid to such a person' (56) mark that sentence as influenced by Yiddish, a language spoken by Miller's family. Critic Mary McCarthy and playwright David Mamet complained that Miller had taken Jewish characters and de-Jewified them in order to have a more universal play. Mamet said of *Salesman*, 'the greatest American play, arguably, is the story of a Jew told by a Jew and cast in "universal" terms. Willy Loman is a Jew in a Jewish industry. But he is never identified as such. His story is never avowed as a Jewish story, and so a great contribution to Jewish American history is lost' (*Michigan Quarterly*: 822). George Ross, reviewing a Yiddish Theatre production in which Joseph Buloff had translated Miller's English into Yiddish, felt as Mamet later would. He believed that 'this Yiddish production is really the original, and the Broadway production was merely—Arthur Miller's translation into English' (*Ross*, 1951: 184).

Obviously Miller did want a play about America and American values, not the problems of a small ethnic group that might be disregarded as unrepresentative. He commented that a touring company, featuring Thomas Mitchell as Willy, Kevin McCarthy (Mary's brother) as Biff, and Darren McGavin as Happy, was received in Boston as 'the best Irish play ever' (Miller, 1987: 322). As Welland says, 'A markedly Jewish Willy Loman might have made the play seem an attack on covert anti-Semitism in American business. By making Willy ethnically neutral Miller emphasizes his point that Willy's trouble is that he is Willy in a particular society, not that he is a Jew, a salesman, or a representative of any other group' (Welland, 1979: 51).

Works Cited

Kauffmann, Stanley (1976), *Persons of the Drama: Theater Criticism and Comment*. New York: Harper & Row.

McCarthy, Mary (1956), 'Introduction,' *Sights and Spectacles, 1937–1956*. New York: Farrar, Straus, and Cuddahy, ix–xvi.

Mamet, David (1998), quoted in *Michigan Quarterly Review*, 37 (Fall 1998), 822.

Miller, Arthur (1984), *Salesman in Beijing*. New York: Viking.

——— (1987), *Timebends*. New York: Grove Press.

Parker, Brian (1988), 'Point of View in Arthur Miller's *Death of a Salesman*,' in Bloom, *Modern Critical Interpretations*, 25–38.

Ross, George (1951), '*Death of a Salesman* in the Original,' *Commentary* 11, 184–6.

Welland, Dennis (1979), *Miller: The Playwright*. London: Methuen.

Works by Arthur Miller

Situation Normal, 1944.

Focus, 1945.

All My Sons, 1947.

Death of a Salesman: Certain Private Conversations in Two Acts and a Requiem, 1949.

An Enemy of the People by Henrik Ibsen (adaptor), 1951.

The Crucible, 1953.

A View from the Bridge (with *A Memory of Two Mondays*): Two One-Act Plays, 1955.

Collected Plays, 1957–81. 2 vols.

The Misfits, 1961.

Jane's Blanket, 1963.

After the Fall, 1964.

Incident at Vichy, 1965.

I Don't Need You Anymore: Stories, 1967, 1987 (as *The Misfits and Other Stories*).

The Price, 1968.

In Russia (with Inge Morath), 1969.

The Portable Arthur Miller. Ed. Harold Clurman, 1971.

The Creation of the World and Other Business, 1973.

In the Country (with Inge Morath), 1977.

Theatre Essays. Ed. Robert A. Martin, 1978.

Chinese Encounters (with Inge Morath), 1979.

Eight Plays, 1981.

Playing for Time: A Screenplay, 1981.

The American Clock, 1982.

Elegy for a Lady, 1982.

Some Kind of Love Story, 1983.

The Archbishop's Ceiling, 1984.

Two-Way Mirror: A Double-Bill Elegy for a Lady and Some Kind of Love Story, 1984.

Playing for Time: A Full-Length Stage Play, 1985.

"Salesman" in Beijing, 1984.

Danger: Memory! A Double-Bill of I Can't Remember Anything and Clara, 1986.

Timebends: A Life, 1987.

Conversations with Arthur Miller. Ed. Matthew C. Roudané, 1987.

Plays: One, 1988.

The Archbishop's Ceiling; The American Clock, 1988.

Plays: Two, 1988.

The Golden Years and The Man Who Had All the Luck, 1989.

Early Plays, 1989.

On Censorship and Laughter, 1990.

Plays: Three, 1990.

Everybody Wins: A Screenplay, 1990.

The Last Yankee, 1991.

The Ride Down Mount Morgan, 1991.

Homely Girl: A Life (with Louis Bourgeois), 1992. 2 vols.

Broken Glass, 1994.

The Last Yankee; with a New Essay, About Theatre Language; and Broken Glass, 1994.

Plays: Four, 1994.

Arthur Miller: An Interview. BBC, 1997.

Mr. Peter's Connections, 1999.

Echoes Down the Corridor: Collected Essays, 1947–2000. Ed. Steven R. Centola, 2000.

On Politics and the Art of Acting, 2001.

Annotated Bibliography

Bhatia, Santosh K. *Arthur Miller: Social Drama as Tragedy*. New Delhi: Arnold-Heinemann Publishers, 1985.

An Indian scholar, Bhatia takes on the concept of tragedy in both its Greek and Shakespearean forms. He begins by listing the five essential elements of tragedy—conflict, suffering, tragic irony, awakening, and metaphysical consideration. In his study of six Miller plays—*Death of a Salesman* among them—he focuses on the way each involves a social issue while conforming to the traditional characteristics of tragedy.

Bigsby, Christopher. *Arthur Miller: 1915–1962*. Cambridge: Harvard University Press, 2009.

Bigsby has published other works on Arthur Miller, but this volume (739 pages) is his most ambitious despite its intended focus on the first half of Miller's life. The author is writing as much as a historian as he is a literary critic: He believes Miller's developing relationship with his country—troubled, triumphant, painful, and reverent—reveals important enduring truths about U.S. history, politics, and culture. Bigsby gives a detailed picture of Miller's early influences in his years in Harlem and Brooklyn and his college years at the University of Michigan. In addition to chapters on five of his most important plays, there is a chapter each devoted to his marriages to Marilyn Monroe and Inge Morath and one to his harassment by Joseph McCarthy and the infamous House Un-American Activities Committee.

Belkin, Ahuva, ed. *Jewish Theatre: Tradition in Transition and Intercultural Vistas*. Tel Aviv: Assaph Book Series, 2008.

This volume of essays looks at Jewish histrionic art from the perspective of multiple and varied cultural traditions within Judaism. An analysis of *Death of a Salesman* is included in a chapter on the topic of "the sins of the fathers" and third-generation American Jewish playwrights. Many critics have detected Jewish themes in *Death of a Salesman*.

Brater, Enoch. *Arthur Miller: A Playwright's Life and Work.* London: Thames & Hudson, 2005.

This volume is distinguished by the inclusion of 70 black-and-white photographs from various stage productions of Miller's work and his personal life and marriages.

—————, ed. *Arthur Miller's Global Theater.* Ann Arbor: University of Michigan Press, 2007.

Plays by Arthur Miller have been performed all over the world, and this volume devotes a chapter to the most significant of these events. One of the most unusual stagings was a performance by the Beijing People's Art Theater of *Death of a Salesman* in 1983. Miller traveled with his wife Inge to select the Chinese actors and direct the play. *Salesman in Beijing* (1984) is Miller's account of that experience, and a chapter about it also appears in this volume.

—————, ed. *Arthur Miller's America: Theater and Culture in a Time of Change.* Ann Arbor: University of Michigan Press, 2005.

The collection of essays in this volume was the result of a symposium on the works and influence of Arthur Miller sponsored by the University of Michigan at Ann Arbor where Miller did his undergraduate work. New insights about the plays and his personal life are included. Miller was unable to make the personal appearance he had hoped for because of an injury, but the university, in order to make its tribute to Miller complete, organized a live video hookup at Miller's Connecticut residence.

Carson, Neil. *Modern Dramatists: Arthur Miller.* New York: St Martin's Press, 1982.

Following two chapters of biographical material, Carson devotes a chapter to each of Miller's plays and one to his nontheatrical writing. Writing about *Death of a Salesman*, Carson emphasizes the three generations of the Loman family, showing parallels and divergences. He offers an interesting look at the impact on audiences of the play's stage design and treatment of time. The book includes several photographs from play performances.

Demastes, William W. and Iris Smith Fischer, eds. *Interrogating America Through Theatre and Performance.* New York: Palgrave Macmillan, 2007.

This volume of essays addresses the perennial questions about our national and cultural identity by looking at the way issues relating to slavery and the assault on Native Americas were first dramatized. There is one chapter on Arthur Miller and *Death of a Salesman*—a comparison with another play about the American Dream. Several illustrations related to theatrical performances add interest to this study.

Hays, Peter L. with Kent Nicholson. *Arthur Miller's "Death of a Salesman."* London: Continuum, 2008

This small volume is part of a British series, Continuum Modern Theatre Guides, that provides a new reader with information on the play's background and context, some recent commentary and analysis, and its production history. An unusual feature is a section called "Workshopping the Play," a series of intellectual and dramatic exercises intended for readers interested in the logistics of producing the play.

Marino, Stephen A., ed. *"The 'Salesman' has a Birthday": Essays Celebrating the Fiftieth Anniversary of Arthur Miller's 'Death of a Salesman.'* Lanham, MD; New York; Oxford: University Press of America, Inc., 2000.

In his preface to this book, compiled to honor the 50th anniversary of Miller's best-known play, editor Stephen A. Marino provides a comment made by the playwright a year after its first performance: "So what is there to feel on this anniversary? Hope, for I now know that people want to listen. A little fear that they want to listen so badly" (vii). People are still listening after 50 years, and the assembled, easily accessible essays discuss why this is so.

Mason, Jeffrey D. *Stone Tower: The Political Theater of Arthur Miller.* Ann Arbor: University of Michigan Press, 2008.

Mason introduces his book with an explanation of the origins and significance of its title. The image of a "blasted stone tower" appears prominently on the stage of Miller's play *After the Fall*. It is described as standing on the site of a German concentration camp and signifies oppressive power, force, allegiance, conflict, and destruction. Mason explains that he chose this symbol to emphasize those central concerns and experiences in Miller's politically engaged life. Many critics have been appropriately preoccupied with the social issues dramatized in the plays, but Mason makes the important distinction between social and political issues, viewing Miller as an artist who—among other things—was concerned with and successful at raising awareness of the serious political trends of the times.

Miller, Arthur. *Timebends*. New York: Grove Press, 1987.

Timebends: A Life is Miller's famous effort to describe his life and works, an autobiography with history and social and political commentary. Published in 1987, it covers only part of his life. The writing is always animated and accessible. Particularly interesting are Miller's reports on how he imagined and then prepared for writing his plays. For example, he gives an intimate account of his changing relationship with director Elia Kazan and his wife, Molly, before, during, and after the HUAC hearings and the phenomenon known as blacklisting.

———. *Salesman in Beijing*. New York: Viking Press, 1984.

This volume contains the log Miller kept each day while rehearsing *Death of a Salesman* in Beijing. Readers interested in China, Chinese/American relations, cultural differences, Arthur Miller, and/or the effects of the Cultural Revolution on Chinese artists and intellectuals would find this account useful. Miller was accompanied by his wife Inge Morath who spoke Chinese and took the numerous photographs of the play in progress included in the book.

Contributors

Harold Bloom is Sterling Professor of the Humanities at Yale University. Educated at Cornell and Yale universities, he is the author of more than 30 books, including *Shelley's Mythmaking* (1959), *The Visionary Company* (1961), *Blake's Apocalypse* (1963), *Yeats* (1970), *The Anxiety of Influence* (1973), *A Map of Misreading* (1975), *Kabbalah and Criticism* (1975), *Agon: Toward a Theory of Revisionism* (1982), *The American Religion* (1992), *The Western Canon* (1994), *Omens of Millennium: The Gnosis of Angels, Dreams, and Resurrection* (1996), *Shakespeare: The Invention of the Human* (1998), *How to Read and Why* (2000), *Genius: A Mosaic of One Hundred Exemplary Creative Minds* (2002), *Hamlet: Poem Unlimited* (2003), *Where Shall Wisdom Be Found?* (2004), and *Jesus and Yahweh: The Names Divine* (2005). In addition, he is the author of hundreds of articles, reviews, and editorial introductions. In 1999, Professor Bloom received the American Academy of Arts and Letters' Gold Medal for Criticism. He has also received the International Prize of Catalonia, the Alfonso Reyes Prize of Mexico, and the Hans Christian Andersen Bicentennial Prize of Denmark.

Arthur Miller (1915–2005) is America's best-known and most prolific playwright. It has been calculated that his most popular play, *Death of a Salesman*, is being performed somewhere in the world every day. Miller was a politically active citizen and during the 1950s endured harassment from Senator Joseph McCarthy and his infamous House Un-American Activities Committee. In the 1960s, he joined other prominent citizens to protest the American war in Vietnam.

George P. Castellitto is professor of English at Felician College in New Jersey, where he is also director of the graduate program in English. In addition to his work on Miller, Castellitto has published essays on the use of images in the work of William Carlos Williams, Wallace Stevens, and Martin Scorsese.

Steven R. Centola (1944–2000) was the founder of the Arthur Miller Society and a renowned Arthur Miller scholar during his professional life. He taught English at Millersville University in Pennsylvania. Among his many publications are *The Achievement of Arthur Miller: New Essays*, and two books written in collaboration with Arthur Miller: *The Theater Essays of Arthur Miller* and *Echoes Down the Corridor: Collected Essays 1944–2000*.

Terry W. Thompson is assistant professor of English at Georgia Southern University.

Dana Kinnison teaches literature and composition at the University of Missouri.

Enoch Brater is professor of dramatic literature at the University of Michigan. He has published three works about Arthur Miller—author of *Arthur Miller: A Playwright's Life and Works* (2005) and editor of *Arthur Miller's America: Theater & Culture in a Time of Change* (2005) and *Arthur Miller's Global Theatre* (2007). Brater has also written about playwright Samuel Beckett.

Deborah R. Geis is professor of English at DePauw University. She is the editor of *Considering Maus: Approaches to Art Spiegelman's "Survivor's Tale" of the Holocaust;* co-editor of *Approaching the Millennium: Essays on Angels in America;* and author of *Postmodern Theatric(k)s: Monologue in Contemporary American Drama*.

Austin E. Quigley is the author of *The Modern Stage and Other Worlds* and *The Pinter Problem*. He is a professor of English at Columbia University and dean of Columbia College.

Gary Harrington teaches in the English department at the Fulton School of Liberal Arts, which is part of Salisbury University in Maryland.

Peter L. Hays is professor emeritus at the University of California at Davis. He has also written about Hemingway's *The Sun Also Rises*.

Acknowledgments

Arthur Miller, *Timebends*, pp. 182–85, 187–93. Published by Grove Press. Copyright © 1987 by Arthur Miller.

George P. Castellitto, "Willy Loman: The Tension Between Marxism and Capitalism." From *"The* Salesman *Has a Birthday" Essays Celebrating the Fiftieth Anniversary of Arthur Miller's* Death of a Salesman, edited by Stephen A. Marino, pp. 79–86. Copyright © 2000 by University Press of America.

Steven R. Centola, "'The Condition of Tension.'" From *"The* Salesman *Has a Birthday" Essays Celebrating the Fiftieth Anniversary of Arthur Miller's* Death of a Salesman, edited by Stephen A. Marino, pp. 55–62. Copyright © 2000 by University Press of America.

Terry W. Thompson, "The Ironic Hercules Reference in *Death of a Salesman.*" From *English Language Notes* 40, no. 4 (June 2003): 73–77. Copyright © 2003 Regents of the University of Colorado.

Dana Kinnison, "Redefining Female Absence in Arthur Miller's *Death of a Salesman* (1949)." From *Women in Literature: Reading Through the Lens of Gender*, edited by Jerilyn Fisher and Ellen S. Silber, pp. 88–90. Published by Greenwood Press. Copyright © 2003 by Jerilyn Fisher and Ellen S. Silber.

Enoch Brater, *Arthur Miller: A Playwright's Life and Works*, pp. 42–46. Copyright © 2005 Thames & Hudson.

Deborah R. Geis, "In Willy Loman's Garden: Contemporary Re-vision of *Death of a Salesman.*" From *Arthur Miller's America: Theater & Culture in a Time of Change*, pp. 202–06, 217. Copyright © by the University of Michigan 2005.

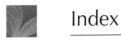

Index

Index